RUNNING
AROUND
THE
WORLD

HOW I RAN
7 MARATHONS ON
7 CONTINENTS IN
7 DAYS

SUSANNAH GILL
WORLD RECORD HOLDER

WITH MIKE ANTONIADES

Praise

'A very inspiring and truly impressive adventure!'
— **Frank Keogh**, BBC sports journalist

'This book shows the determination and dedication needed to compete in such an incredibly tough challenge, a massive achievement. It's great insight on how to tackle a multi-day challenge!'
— **Mimi Anderson**, endurance athlete and multiple Guinness World Record holder

'Susannah was a really strong World Marathon Challenge competitor and her World Record is a really great achievement for an amateur runner.'
— **Michael Wardian**, male World Marathon Challenge record holder

'Grit and determination don't cover it. Susannah's world record transcended the world of endurance sport into the popular psyche. A true warrior.'
— **George Nash**, GB Olympic gold medalist, Rio Games 2016

'Susannah is an incredible ambassador for women's running. Anyone interested in running at any level will be inspired by this book.'
— **Esther Newman**, Editor, *Women's Running* magazine

'2019's Inspiration in Running is just that! Our award winner Susannah proves to us all that we can take great enjoyment from running whilst inspiring others along the way.'
— **Sam Corrick**, Editor, The Running Awards

'Sport requires great physical fitness but also significant mental toughness. This book is a fantastic insight into how Susannah took on and conquered a truly unique challenge.'
— **Michael Caulfield**, leading sports psychology consultant

'This book is a "must read" for anyone interested in amazing stories of human achievement. The old adage of ordinary people doing extraordinary things simply doesn't do justice to Susannah. Sure, there'll be some hacks and top tips for runners, but more than anything, you'll be inspired and uplifted.'
— **Tim Lawler**, Chief Executive, SportsAid

'As every runner knows, running is about more than putting one foot in front of the other; it is about our lifestyle and who we are.'
— **Joan Benoit Samuelson**, winner of the first ever women's Olympic marathon in 1984

R∃THINK PRESS

Contents

Foreword

If there is a moral to be taken out of every story, the lesson I must take from this tale of endeavour is be careful how you use your bragging rights.

Ten years ago, I thought of myself as an experienced enough marathon runner to offer people a few tips. Two runs in London, another two in New York and one in Paris gave me a decent level of knowledge – all achieved without too much training, and in what seemed respectable-enough times. A 3:36 in the Big Apple followed by a 3:35 back at home, and a sub three-and-a-half seemed within my sights if only I had the inclination.

It was with that track record that I goaded my then Executive Assistant as she limbered up for her first – and possibly last – attempt over 26.2 miles. The office banter over Christmas was all about how she – thirteen years my junior – would fare against the yardstick I had set. Bet you won't beat me; bet you I will. You can see how it was panning out.

So, her arrival back in the office one January morning in 2009, having completed Gloucester in the more than reasonable 3:46, led me to have a field day. Ten minutes was not much – particularly given that hers had been a first outing – but it was quite enough. I was quicker, and Susannah was not going to be allowed to forget it.

That position of ascendancy didn't last long. By April she was two minutes quicker than my best, having completed London. Then wind forward ten years to see how much you can be made to look a turkey. My marathon numbers have gone up by one – Athens in 2018 – while my time has slipped by almost an hour. And hers? Now well through sixty marathons in total, including a world record in a peacock costume, ultras for fun, five marathons of standard length under 3 hours – and the phenomenal achievement about which this book is the subject: 7 marathons on 7 continents in 7 days – in world record time.

The tale of how she got there is one of dedication, commitment, resilience and grit – as well as an object lesson in how you can transform performance with the right technique and approach. Susannah was not, when I met her, an obvious marathon runner; and her hobbling arrival back in the office that Monday morning never suggested she was about to become one. Today she is, at the age of 35, one of the most consistent non-professional performers in sport – as well as a picture of health, happiness and determination, carrying all the benefits that sport brings into her everyday (both professional and personal) life.

This is an inspiring story, because it shows in its way that anyone can do it. You will need some of the bloody-mindedness that was apparent in her when she first turned up for a job interview, but after that you can add the ingredients to suit. It almost inspires me to attempt a return to the fray at my grand old age and try to break that 3:30 milestone at last. But let's not get totally carried away.

Mark Davies,
Chair, British Rowing

Introduction
Why We Wrote This Book

I do not know the moment I first said to myself 'I am a runner' but I am now most definitely a runner. I am not the best runner in the world, but I am a runner and it's one of the ways I define myself. Probably the main way.

I would rather talk about running than almost anything else. Its wonderful simplicity and yet endless complexities fascinate me. Regardless of experience there is always more to learn about running. The simple act of putting one foot in front of the other can fill a void like nothing else I know.

It's also filled a lifetime of fascination for Mike, who knows more about how the body moves than probably anyone else in the world. He has worked with professionals, amateurs, Olympians, long-distance runners, sprinters, footballers, rowers, the very young and the very old. Mike's expertise, advice and support are simply the best.

Yet, until 2019, he'd never trained anyone to run seven marathons on seven continents in seven days, making this a new experience for both of us. We wanted to write this book together to show how, with the right approach, the seemingly impossible can in fact become perfectly possible.

The World Marathon Challenge was the definition of a team effort, as the vast majority of achievements are. Regardless of what challenge you want to take on, we hope you find this book helpful and inspiring in equal measure. We really can all be amazing.

Happy reading... and even happier running!

Susanah Mike

PART ONE
BECOMING A RUNNER

1
The Education Years

Running is now a central part of my life. I do it nearly every day of the year. Like many runners, I simply can't imagine a life where I do not run.

At school I was into sport, but not excessively so. I enjoyed netball and hockey and in the summer months I was part of the athletics squad, taking on a diverse range of events from shotput to the relay team.

I was fifteen when I went on my first ever 'run'. It wasn't because I suddenly wanted to run, but more that I needed to get fit. I have ridden horses all my life and was lucky enough to have a lovely big kind horse called Dylon. At the end of our first cross-country round at a one-day event, we were both puffing and sweating so much it was clear that fitness was an issue for horse and rider.

We lived on a small farm in Shropshire and after school, to increase my fitness, I started walking around the fields, until one day when I broke into a run. It was really hard work running on uneven grass and I would only go around a couple of fields at a time before feeling exhausted. However, it started to make a difference. I started to get fitter and even began to enjoy it, appreciating the space and fresh air after a day at school before tackling homework. I didn't know then how important running on the Shropshire hills would become for me.

At the University of Exeter, I indulged in the classic university lifestyle until I took up rowing in my second year as something interesting to do. I loved rowing and met some committed fellow rowers – men and women. We had a great team approach at the University Boat Club and won a few pots and medals along the way in various regattas. That made it all the more worthwhile but, just as importantly, we had a lot of fun.

Joining the world of work

After graduating, I was lucky enough to land my dream job as a researcher in Westminster. As someone who loves politics, this could not have been more exciting and led me into a new life in one of the world's finest cities.

I lived in Clapham South with access to Clapham Common, still a favourite running location. I could also go to the gym in Westminster, but I only troubled to do either occasionally. I was much more likely to be found at the bar drinking white wine and going to bed far too late on a work night. In Westminster, as a young researcher, you drank on a Tuesday because it wasn't a Monday and you drank on a Thursday because, hopefully, there wasn't too much to do on a Friday. If you add in the weekends, that's a significant part of the week taken up with drinking and socialising. Don't get me wrong, I enjoyed it, but equally I knew it wasn't really me. I was getting a bit squishy about the edges, weighing over 12 stone, and I didn't feel especially fulfilled.

I moved jobs and joined Betfair. This turned out to be an unexpected but great career move for lots of reasons. I worked for the managing director, Mark Davies, now chair of British Rowing, as his executive assistant and researcher. I was able to experience the business world for the first time in a fun and dynamic company. On top of that we were based at Hammersmith, so when time allowed a few of us would head out for a lunchtime run along the river. We'd go up to Barnes, then over the bridge and down to Putney, and return to the office a bit pink and incredibly cheerful. A quick shower and a sandwich at the desk and I would be ready for the afternoon.

Just before joining Betfair I had decided I wanted to run the London Marathon. Like everyone else, I would watch the world's biggest marathon on TV and be inspired by the sights and sounds of this truly unique event. I got a place through Help the Aged (now Age Concern) and set about training in the summer of 2008 with the ambition of running the 2009 marathon.

My first marathon

At some point I must have had a wobble about running the London Marathon, especially as I was asking for sponsorship from friends and family to cover my charity place. In order to deal with this I decided I should run a 'practice marathon' in Gloucester at the end of January to see if I could really manage 26.2 miles in one go.

Up until that stage none of my family had taken it at all seriously that I would really go out and run a marathon. The weekend before the race, dad asked me how I was going to get to and from the Gloucester. I said I would drive. Dad didn't feel happy with the thought of me driving after a marathon so agreed to drive me down, stay and watch the race, and then drop me at the train station after so I could get back to London.

It turned out this was a good move. I can't believe dad really enjoyed the 3:46 he had to stand out in the cold watching me complete the three-loop course, but I was very glad I didn't have to drive afterwards. Running your first marathon is a truly bizarre experience for mind and body. In asking your body to do something it has never done before you simply do not know how it is going to react. In my case I felt very sick when I stopped running, a feeling that did not pass for a couple of hours and only improved on eating a marmite sandwich. My hips were really sore and I felt like I had golf ball sized blisters on my feet. But I loved it.

I was very lame for two or three days, with everything south of my waist feeling tight and sore. My legs felt like they would never run again, but slowly and surely I got back on the cross trainer and then was back out running a few days later. By the time April came around I felt as ready for the London marathon as I was ever going to be.

My first London Marathon

The London Marathon is an experience you never forget. From the expo at the Excel Centre where you collect your number to the train out to Blackheath on the morning of the race, the whole thing is packed with sights, sounds, smells (mainly Deep Heat) and a lot of other people.

Like most runners I had a sleepless night before the race, tossing and turning, and felt relieved to get up at 6am to start the day. It took me nearly a decade of marathon running to learn to sleep properly the night before a race, and I still get plenty of pre-race nerves, especially ahead of London each year.

I can remember everything before my first London Marathon and definitely the hobbling home afterwards; slowly down the river with my kit bag over my shoulder. But oddly I can't remember much about the race itself; everything must have passed in a blur. Mark had a bet with me that I could not beat his time of 3:36 so all I can remember is being very satisfied when I crossed the line in 3:34.

It was wonderful to head into the office the next day, albeit slowly, and thank colleagues for their donations. With the endorphins masking the pain of sore muscles and blisters, I decided I wanted to run more marathons. By the end of the week I had entered the Berlin Marathon for the following September, and I was on a mission to run a marathon in under three and a half hours.

Getting into my stride

What I thought was a straightforward target turned into a bit of a saga.

I messed up the timing in Berlin that year by starting too far back and being held up by slower runners, and so finished in 3:33. The following spring, London came around again and I was lucky enough to get a ballot place. But I got stuck in Stockholm on a work trip for ten days after the Icelandic volcano Eyjafjallajökull erupted for the first time in 200 years and grounded all European flights. I finally got home on the Wednesday before the London Marathon after taking half a dozen trains through Europe over the previous thirty-six hours. Needless to say, I was tired and not in great shape to run a marathon, but I managed another 3:33 effort.

By this stage I was starting to get frustrated, so I entered the Amsterdam Marathon for the following October. Finally, on my third attempt, I nailed it in 3:28.

Running constantly reminds us how hard we need to work to achieve our goals. It requires some serious dedication and willingness to commit time and energy. I now look back on this early running achievement as one of my most satisfying. I did it with no help or support and yet, through sheer determination and persistence, I got better.

More marathons

Once I had broken the 3:30 barrier, I got a new wave of confidence. I would run three or four marathons a year, with my training consisting of post-work gym sessions and the lunchtime runs, on top of longer runs at the weekend over the hills of Shropshire. I did virtually no strength work and there was no great science behind my training.

One thing I did learn was that I loved to go out and race. When I was surrounded by other people, I could run so much quicker than when plodding along by myself. Every year my London Marathon time came down. In 2012 the Animal Health Trust kindly gave me a place and, as something a bit different, I decided to see if I could break the Guinness world record for the fastest woman dressed as an animal. The record was 3:38, so I knew I could do it if I chose a sensible costume. I found a peacock costume which was relatively lightweight, with a large tail being the only significant accessory. I practised running in it the weekend before the race. I had to use some extra elastic to keep the tail in place, but I was otherwise happy with it.

It turned out that the tail had a beneficial and unexpected use. As it stuck out behind me it stopped anyone getting too close to me, eliminating the chance of any heel-tripping in the early miles, which is always a hazard. I crossed the line in 3:18, setting a new record. I held that record until 2016, when I was beaten by a tortoise!

Breaking the three-hour marathon barrier

I was now a regular marathon runner. I had run London six times, along with Berlin, Amsterdam,

Dublin (twice), Stockholm, New York, and more unusual ones like the Great Wall of China.

As well as marathons, I was running some ultra-marathons. This started with a couple of straight-forward 35- and 40-mile races and progressed to the tougher 100-mile races. I ran a 100-kilometre Pharaonic Race in Egypt, which finished at the Pyramids. I even did a 24-hour race around Gosforth Park near Newcastle, which I won outright by covering 170 kilometres (105 miles).

By January 2015 I had got my marathon time down to 3:06, which I achieved in Dubai. I never felt I would be a sub-three-hour marathon runner and certainly didn't go out to break that barrier, but at the London Marathon in April 2015 I did just that. As I crossed the line with the clock reading 2:58:51, I don't remember feeling happy – just a bit stunned.

Within ten minutes of finishing I realised all was not well. After collecting my bag, I tried to put my track-suit bottoms on and realised I could not bend my right knee. Not only that, but it was sore. Even through the heady mix of endorphins and a new best time, I had to acknowledge I was in some discomfort. I finally man-aged to get my tracksuit bottoms on by sitting on the floor and wandered off slowly to meet some friends in the pub. I hoped my knee just needed some rest.

2
The Injury Years

Unfortunately, my injured knee needed more than rest. Every time I attempted a run, I could make it no more than half a mile down the road before coming to a grinding halt as sharp pains shot through my knee. After two months, I eventually gave in and went to the doctor, who referred me for an MRI scan. The scan showed cartilage damage between the two bones in the joint: bone was rubbing on bone. The acute shooting pain was caused by bits of broken-off cartilage floating around my knee and getting stuck, like eggshell, in places they should not have been.

I felt more positive now I knew what the problem was, but by this stage I was not using my right leg properly. The muscle wastage was clear; my right quadricep had got smaller and weaker. I was lucky to have private medical insurance through work, which allowed me to receive weekly physio sessions. These sessions helped to stabilise my right leg and were crucial for my morale.

The doctors wanted to do an operation that involved taking stem cells from my hip and inserting them into my knee. There, they might grow back as cartilage and replace what had been lost. This was a new operation at the time, and the insurance company said they would not pay for it. After endless frustrating calls, I gave up arguing and headed to Stanmore for an NHS appointment at the Royal National Orthopaedic Hospital. The doctor said he would happily do the stem cell operation, as he was interested to see how it would work on a young, fit patient. Alternatively, he could simply take out the bits of cartilage that were floating around my knee and see if things settled down of their own accord.

The second approach, known as an arthroscopy, had the huge advantage of being straightforward keyhole surgery. It could be done in a day and I would be able to walk out of the hospital. If I had the stem cell surgery, I would not able to bear weight on my right leg for six weeks. By now 9 months has passed I was feeling frustrated and wanted to get moving again, so we decided to go with the arthroscopy and see what happened.

I cannot thank the NHS enough for looking after me; everyone was so helpful and kind. The operation went smoothly and within a few days I was back on the cross-trainer. Once the stitches were out of my knee, I could try some short runs. I found I was pain-free, and despite losing some fitness, I was back in the game of running and feeling much happier.

Getting back to running marathons

Four months after the operation, which I'd had in July 2016, I went out to Athens to run the world's classic marathon. My right hamstring cramped at 28 kilometres into the race due to lack of strength and fitness, but I still got home in 3:17. I knew I was still a marathon runner.

In 2017, I clocked a new best time of 2:58:02 in London. That summer, I thought I would have some fun doing some off-road marathons. I am no fan of running through mud, as I find it hard to get into a rhythm. It also hugely increases my chances of falling over, as happened at the end of the South Downs Marathon. Just 500 metres from the finish line, I caught my toe on a stone and went down like an elephant. I landed face down, hitting my nose hard enough to start a nose-bleed. My hands and knees were covered in blood, and everything was stinging. I got up and crossed the line to win the race, looking a complete mess.

Although I was still enjoying running, I knew I was not running well and needed some help to improve. I just had no idea where to turn.

Finding The Running School

I had never planned to take running seriously enough to need any professional support or coaching. I liked reading a good blog or article as much as the next runner, but that's a big step away from working with someone on a one-to-one basis.

In the running community, social media – especially Twitter and Instagram – is an enormously helpful source of information. So many people are passionate about running and are willing to share their thoughts and ideas for us all to learn from. I loved exploring a rabbit warren of posts, links and articles that gave me nuggets of information about training and races I might otherwise never have found.

During one of these scrolling sessions, I came across the Twitter account @RunningSchool. I went to their website, which said that they were 'movement, rehabilitation and speed specialists dedicated to helping you achieve your goals'. My goal was simply not to fall over, so I signed up for six Running Technique sessions.

From my first session onwards, my approach to running completely changed. First, they put me on the treadmill and wondered out loud how I had managed to run marathons in under three hours with my current technique. Then they put me on a mat with lots of squares and symbols to begin some footwork exercises. These exercises are the basics of reforming how we move, from the feet upwards.

Over the next six sessions I learned plenty of these 'dynamic movement skills' (DMS).

MIKE ON DMS

DMS is a training and rehabilitation method that stimulates the proprioceptive system which is our body's interaction with the ground. The DMS method helps to refine and develop neuromuscular efficiency and change motor patterns to make movement more efficient. I use it with runners and performance athletes to improve their interaction with the ground and their foot speed.

I also use DMS for rehabilitation after an injury to rebuild movement patterns and improve symmetry and synchronisation in both sides of the body. This leads to better coordination, balance, and rhythm. These skills ultimately help to increase movement competence and confidence in functional movement during rehabilitation and helps with speed and agility.

For more information about DMS visit: www.movementskills.co.uk/

DMS is hard work. It's physically and mentally draining, as you're changing how your body moves. I would finish sessions feeling like a zombie, but I also felt satisfied because I was becoming a better runner.

These are the crucial things I learned in the early days with The Running School:

- **Glutes and hamstrings:** I now lift my heels up and have a clear 'running cycle' with my legs. That means I am making my glutes and hamstrings do most of the work, which takes the strain off my quads and knees.

- **Feet:** I now place my feet on two clear tracks rather than letting them cross over as many runners do. By letting your feet cross over, you increase the chances of tripping yourself up – something I was good at doing. You also make your hips, knees and feet work at an angle, rather than in a straight line as they are built to do. This was probably one reason I ended up damaging my right knee.

- **Core:** I am now much more upright and stronger in my core. A strong core helps you maintain your posture and reduces the chances of falling over.

- **Arms:** I now make far better use of my arms. Running is a leg-based exercise, but the rhythm comes entirely from your arms. When you're tired, your arms become a vital way of maintaining your pace. If your arms can work like pistons by your side, your legs will follow, allowing you to maintain a higher speed. I am now better at doing this in the final stages of a marathon.

3

Signing up to the World Marathon Challenge

Once I was back on the road and feeling more confident about my running, I was ready for the next challenge. I just needed to decide what it would be.

I had heard about the '7 marathons on 7 continents in 7 days' challenge way back when I started running. It had first been completed by the legendary Sir Ranulph Fiennes, although he ran the 'Antarctica leg' on the Falkland Islands. I thought it had a beautiful symmetry, being that there are seven days in a week and seven continents, with humans clever enough to be able to get to all these places in 168 hours.

It was not until January 2018, when I came across the company World Marathon Challenge, that I considered taking it on. Before the company existed, runners had to complete the feat using commercial airlines and organising all the races themselves: a tough task. World Marathon Challenge takes care of all the organisation, which makes it more accessible.

Without telling anyone, I sent an enquiry email. When I got a reply from race organiser Richard Donovan, I completed the list of questions about my personality and running experience. Much to my surprise, he was willing to give me a place. I was far from ready to commit and spent the whole summer throwing the idea around in my head.

A large part of me thought it was the silliest idea in the world. It would be expensive and, crucially, it could easily end in failure: I had never run more than one marathon in three weeks, let alone seven in one week. Despite feeling much better and stronger because of working with The Running School, I had already had one knee operation so I was far from indestructible.

But my gut instinct told me to go for it. If I didn't sign up, I would regret it for years to come. At age thirty-four, I was probably in the best shape I would ever be in. And I was sensible enough to know that if I signed up, I would need a proper training programme to get fit enough and stay free of injury.

I turned to the only person I knew who could help. In late August 2018, I called The Running School and asked to speak to Mike. When he called me back twenty minutes later, we had a short conversation that would change my life forever.

After waffling for a bit, I told Mike that I had the opportunity to do something I had always wanted to do – to run seven marathons on seven continents in seven days – and that my one question was 'If I sign up, will you coach me?' There was a pause for one second, and then all I remember hearing Mike reply was 'OK'. In that single moment, I allowed myself to mentally commit to the World Marathon Challenge and to believe for the first time that I might really attempt it.

Mike's initial answer was followed by lots of caveats and details about how we would need to work on a specific programme, which would include plenty of very long runs. I would need to come to The Running School every week for lessons, and it would be physically and mentally tough. Crucially, he said that from what he had seen he believed I could do it. Whether Mike believed this or not was irrelevant: in his quiet and understated way, he made me believe I could do it, and that was the vital first step.

With just over five months to go until the start of the World Marathon Challenge, I was ready to embrace a brave new world of training to prepare for the challenge of a lifetime.

4
Mike On Training Susannah

Meeting Susannah

I first met Susannah at our HQ in Acton. She was struggling a bit with her running after knee surgery and came to The Running School to see if we could find out why.

First, one of my colleagues did a detailed biomechanical analysis of Susannah's running technique, followed by a functional movement analysis. A biomechanical analysis gives information about how the runner moves day-to-day and their running technique. It helps to identify any inefficiencies that the runner has developed after an injury or out of habit. My colleague asked me to have a look at the video clips to see what I thought.

BEFORE

Susannah is over-striding, rotating the shoulders and landing heavily

Susannah is rotating her feet outwards

Susannah is crossing over her midline of her body with right leg

AFTER

Susannah is now over-striding less, more upright and using her glutes more

Susannah now lifts her feet up vertically and runs on two clear tracks

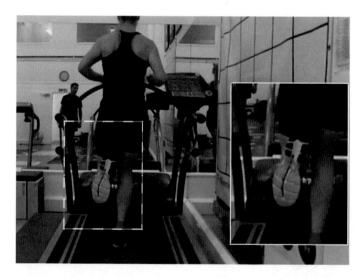

Her left and right are closer to a mirror image of each other

With Susannah's permission, I'll now describe what I saw in her first visit to The Running School.

Two obvious issues jumped out at me. First, Susannah was over-striding on both legs, but more on the left than on the right. Her right leg was rotating in a semi-circle and landing across the midline of her body, which was causing a breaking action on every stride. Her left leg was then compensating by over-striding even further, but also coming perilously close to her right calf muscle. This was almost certainly the cause of her falls!

Second, Susannah was counter-rotating her shoulders rather than using her arms to get forward momentum and rhythm. All these inefficiencies meant that she was wasting a lot of energy. More importantly, by over striding and landing with her feet ahead of her body she was breaking and decelerating with every step.

The tests on Susannah's proprioception (how her feet interact with the ground) showed that her movement was breaking down and she was favouring one leg over the other. This is common with runners who compensate because of pain or a previous injury, continuing to run without doing enough rehabilitation.

The reason for this is simple. The brain and the nervous system work together to keep us moving. If a runner is in pain and starts to compensate or to run slower, the movement pattern in the brain will change gradually. This 'new' permanent inefficient running technique becomes the normal way we move.

Running is a skill that can be taught and developed. Like many recreational runners, Susannah had not been taught to run. My first objective was to change Susannah's running technique to make her more efficient. It took us about eight weeks to change the running cycle to a point where Susannah didn't have to think about her technique when running. It can take longer after injury or surgery for the changes to be effective, but Susannah did her homework and improved quickly.

Coaching Susannah for the World Marathon Challenge

I was coaching when one of my team said Susannah had called and wanted to talk to me about something. I assumed she had picked up a niggle and wanted to discuss rehab or advice on if she could still run.

Having worked with Susannah on her technique after her knee surgery, I knew her as just one of the many athletes my school worked with. I knew she had improved, first with her running technique and then with her speed endurance, but I had not spent much time with her to get to know her as a person.

She seemed pleasant, loved running and, like so many runners, needed running to help her cope with a demanding job.

When I called her back, I remember the conversation going something like this:

Mike: 'How are you doing? Anything wrong?'

Susannah: 'I'm OK, but I want to take on a mad challenge I have always dreamed of doing. I have the chance to take on the World Marathon Challenge, and I wanted to ask you if you would coach me if I signed up.'

I had heard the name of the challenge, but I'd never really thought about what it entailed.

Mike: 'What does it involve?'

Susannah: 'Running seven marathons on seven continents in seven days.'

Mike: 'OK. Oh, that's a bit more difficult than what I assumed from the name! Have you done anything like this before?'

Susannah: 'No. I have done some 100-kilometre and 100-mile races, but without training specifically for them.'

Mike: 'Right. When is it taking place?'

I was thinking that if we had twelve months to get Susannah ready, with a little luck we might avoid any injuries.

Susannah: 'End of January 2019, but the exact dates depend on the weather in Antarctica.'

Mike: 'That's only five months away!'

Susannah: 'I know – that's why I need your help.'

Mike: 'OK, I'll do some research and we can chat more when you're next in about how it will work. We have just over 20 weeks to do this if we're going to work together.'

The thoughts that ran through my brain were that we didn't have enough time. Susannah clearly didn't know how difficult this was going to be, physically and mentally. How fit was she really? It's one thing running a single marathon, but another doing seven in a row. How tough was she?

The one thing I didn't ask when I said I would coach her for the World Marathon Challenge was why she was doing it. You don't ask a runner or an athlete why they want to challenge themselves by doing something most of the population would not even think about doing, let alone spend their money, time and effort on. In my experience, people are either running to get away from something or running to be something. There is also another reason: simply because it's there! Whatever the reason, one thing is for sure – running is great therapy.

I have coached many full-time elite and professional athletes. I have also coached recreational runners, tri-athletes and ultra-runners who have a full-time job but take their sport just as seriously as the professionals do. My experience has taught me that it takes a special character trait to go through the pain of the training, the preparation and the challenge itself. It requires not only physical attributes but also strong mental skills.

I didn't know whether Susannah was running away from something or wanting to be something. Nor did I know if she would be mentally or physically strong enough. But I was immediately intrigued by the challenge. I knew Susannah as client, but I didn't know her character or what I call her 'inner athlete'. Your inner athlete is what determines if you can stick to the training, finish the job and give it your absolute best. If your best is not good enough, that's OK. You know you have given everything you had.

Your inner athlete is not just about self-belief or the motivational words that you say to convince yourself that you can achieve something. It is about having the discipline to do what you know needs to be done, even when you're feeling awful and you could make several excuses to yourself about why you can't do it. It's about digging deep; it's about determination, grit and stubbornness. It's about carrying on when you're so tired that the thought of getting out of bed to train causes you pain. It's about sacrificing your social life and changing your habits: eating well, drinking well and recovering well.

In Susannah's case, it was about being able to do all this while having a full-time job. I didn't know that part of her personality. I wasn't prepared to put in all that time and effort into a partnership without being confident that she would be able to give her all. Coaching is not just about writing a training programme; it's a collaboration and a partnership between athlete and coach. I needed to know Susannah would be as committed as I would be. At this stage I gave a tentative yes, but I had my doubts. I found out pretty quickly that Susannah had grit in abundance!

PART TWO
TRAINING FOR THE WORLD MARATHON CHALLENGE

5
Weeks 1–4:
3 September – 30 September 2018

Mike: Establishing the rules

The first four weeks of the training programme had several physiological objectives and was critical in establishing a coach-athlete relationship. I wanted to:

1. See how Susannah would respond, physically and mentally, to the variety of the training sessions, especially the tough speed-endurance sessions

2. Identify how she would best recover from a block of hard training, stay injury-free and be able to perform in her job

3. Introduce strength training, given most runners dislike or ignore any form of this, preferring to

lace up their trainers and go for a run than to work on specific weaknesses

4. Start to prepare Susannah mentally for the challenge ahead, both the twenty or so weeks of training and the World Marathon Challenge

I gave Susannah a couple of books to read on mental strength and preparation. We reviewed everything each week and made adjustments where necessary.

We also set few rules:

- No alcohol

- Eat well after a training session

- Communicate regularly

Susannah lives in London, so it was relatively easy to schedule a weekly session at The Running School. There, we could debrief on the week's training and sort out any issues with technique.

I give all my athletes a weekly monitoring sheet to complete, which details everything from sleep and nutrition to energy levels and hydration. It gives us a clear picture of what is working and what needs changing.

The coaching role is not just about designing the training sessions. My role was to be honest and truthful, give good advice, and motivate and encourage

Susannah when needed. My overall responsibility was to keep her free from injury and mentally healthy. Endurance running is a good obsession that can become a bad addiction.

Any doubts that I had about Susannah's ability to cope with the challenge quickly disappeared during the first four weeks.

Getting started and agreeing the terms of working together

Although I had been running marathons, and a few ultras, for nearly ten years, I had never followed a training programme. I had read many books and blogs, used my common sense and fitted in training with the practicalities of life. That meant doing long runs at the weekends, when I tended to have more time.

My self-training journey had ended abruptly in 2015 when I injured my knee. Finding The Running School had made me realise the importance of doing strength work alongside running for all-round fitness. But I didn't wear a Garmin so I had no idea what my heart rate was doing when I ran, and I never recorded any information about my training.

Life was about to get very different under Mike's tuition.

Week 1-4	Monday	Tuesday	Wednesday	Thursday	Friday	Saturday	Sunday	Total running/ walking time
1	**Walk:** 20 minutes **Run:** 15 minutes (easy)	**Run:** 40 minutes Strength work: Lower body • squats • straight leg deadlift Upper body • overhead shoulder press • bent over reverse flies • bicep and tricep curls	**Run:** 20 minutes *Intervals:* • Run 1 × 6 minutes • Run 1 × 9 minutes • Run 1 × 6 minutes • Run 1 × 6 minutes (3-minute recovery after each) **Run:** 10 minutes (cool down) Total running time: 69 minutes	Running School session	**Run:** 25 minutes (easy) *Intervals:* • 5 × 1,000m (hard) (3-minute easy run after each) Total running time: 63 minutes (based on 4:30 for 5 × 1,000m pieces)	**Run:** 60 minutes (easy)	**Run/walk for 3 hours:** Run 30 minutes, walk 6 minutes (× 5)	447 minutes (7 hours 27 minutes)
2	**Walk:** 15 minutes **Run:** 25 minutes (easy)	**Run:** 40 minutes (easy) Strength work	**Run:** 20 minutes (warm up) *Intervals:* • 10 × 800m (timed) **Run:** 10 minutes (cool down) Total running time: 70 minutes (based on 4 minute 800m pieces	Running School session	**Run:** 15 minutes (easy) *Intervals:* • Run 5 minutes fast, 2 minutes easy (× 10) **Run:** 15 minutes (easy) Total running time: 100 minutes	**Run:** 60 minutes (easy)	**Run:** 20 minutes (easy) *Intervals:* • Run 5 × 60 seconds (hard) • Run 5 × 45 seconds (hard) • Run 5 × 30 seconds (hard) (60 seconds recovery between each) **Run:** 60 minutes (easy) Total running time: 92 minutes	402 minutes (6 hours, 42 minutes)

3	**Run:** 30 minutes (easy)	**Run:** 40 minutes (medium) Strength work	**Run:** 20 minutes (easy), 40 minutes (marathon pace) **Run:** 10 minutes (cool down) Total running time: 70 minutes	Running School session	**Run:** 20 minutes (easy) Intervals: Run 10 × 1,000m (3-minute jog after each) **Run:** 10-minute (cool down) Total running time: 105 minutes (based on 4:30 minute 1,000m pieces)	Wimbledon Marathon: 3:35	**Run:** 13 miles, half marathon race test time (100 minutes/1 hour 40 minutes) Total running time: 100 minutes	540 minutes (9 hours, 20 minutes)
4	**Run:** 30 minutes (easy)	Strength work	**Run:** 45 minutes (easy)	Running School session	**Run:** 45 minutes (medium)	**Run:** 45 minutes (medium)	**Run** for 3 hours: 30 minutes (easy), 60 minutes (marathon pace), 30 minutes (easy), 60 minutes (marathon pace)	345 minutes (5 hours, 45 minutes)

45

After agreeing to be my coach for the World Marathon Challenge, Mike started as he meant to go on. He changed my approach almost overnight. In our first conversation, he didn't talk about the miles I would run but everything that would sit alongside the running. This was the start of Mike preparing me mentally for the challenge ahead.

These are what he said would be the crucial elements of working together:

Daily monitoring

Just as I would work to a specific programme, I would need to record specific aspects of my life that shaped my overall wellbeing. Mike sent me a spreadsheet with a column for all the things he needed to know. I would record the following information every day and send it to him on a Sunday evening:

- Resting heart rate
- Sleep quality
- Energy levels pre-exercise
- Energy levels post-exercise
- What I had eaten during the day
- Hydration levels
- Exercise session details – what I had done and how it felt

- Maximum heart rate during the exercise session
- Any other information I wanted to share

At first, it was odd and even tedious to record my day in such minute detail. I bought a basic Garmin, so recording my heart rate was easy. Other factors, such as how I felt before and after exercise or the quality of my sleep, were harder. I would sit and think 'How do I feel today?' in a way I had never consciously done previously.

It only took me a couple of weeks to get used to it, but it's a habit that I've kept up as Mike and I continue to train together. Although Mike needed the data to shape the training programme, I am sure he had me filling it in so that I started to be more aware of looking after myself… and it works. These things have a real impact on how well you train. Recording the information makes you much more conscious of looking after your mind and body in a positive way. It's a significant 'nudge factor' in maintaining your wellbeing.

Reading and learning

When I was not running, I was to be reading about running. In our first session, before I stepped on the treadmill, Mike handed me two books. They were so good that I still regularly think about elements of them.

The first was *Grit* by Angela Duckworth, which sets out in an engaging way why passion and resilience are the secrets to success. The second book was *The Art of Mental Training* by DC Gonzalez with Alice McVeigh, which talks about the crucial elements of a 'champion' and the mind set needed to win. Another fascinating read is *Brain Rules* by David Medina, which explains how the brain works and why we think about and do the things we do. By reading you can keep learning, and just as training increases your fitness levels, learning allows you to expand your horizons.

Lifestyle changes

If I was going to fit a serious training programme around work and other commitments in life, some things were going to have to take a back seat. Cleverly, Mike never told me what to do, but his suggestions were so obviously the right thing that I always ended up following them.

The first thing to disappear from my life was alcohol. I wasn't a big drinker, but leave me with a bottle of prosecco or champagne and there wouldn't be much left for anyone else. On a Saturday night with no race the next day, it was good to relax with a drink. But while I was training, the craziest thing I drank for months was a can of sugar-free Lilt or Diet Coke. Once I was in the groove of training, I didn't miss it.

Along with alcohol, I cut back on my social life. Committing to anything after work was tough, as I would need to fit in training somewhere else in the day. Committed as I was, sprint intervals at 6am did not appeal much. I sometimes went out on a Saturday night, but not if I was competing on a Sunday: the alarm would always go off too early. I'm sure hardly anyone noticed, and I still have fantastic friends!

Keeping a diary

Mike advised that aside from my daily monitoring, I should keep a diary. He said that I was undertaking something special, so I should ensure I have a record of how I felt throughout. He added that other people would be interested in what I was doing. I was sceptical but, as I do what Mike tells me, I bought one that said on the cover 'It's not a dream, it's a plan'.

Keeping in close communication

Lastly, Mike said we were to communicate regularly. He wanted to hear from me after races and if anything went wrong in between our training sessions. We all use the expression 'how are you?' but I am not sure we ever really expect an honest answer. Mike was saying that he genuinely wanted to know how I was feeling. That felt enormously supportive, and it's one of the best aspects of having a really good coach.

A slow but steady start

Mike's training programme was far more structured than what I was used to. I remember vividly the treadmill session in the first week, which consisted of short and random amounts of running time with two-minute breaks in between. I had no idea why I was doing this and only asked Mike afterwards. He said it was to break up my usual rhythm during runs and make me do something completely different.

For the same reason, at the weekends he had me doing run/walks, breaking up long runs with short sections of walking. We were working on the assumption that by the latter stages of the World Marathon Challenge I might need to walk sections, so I needed to get used to it now. I find walking boring compared to running, so I was glad when this element of the training was over and I could move on to solid long runs.

At the end of week 3, on Saturday 22 September, I ran the Wimbledon Marathon. This had been in my diary when I started training, but seeing what shape I was in and how I felt afterwards fitted in well with the schedule. The race started in the afternoon, which was unusual, and the day got wetter and wetter. The fourth lap around Wimbledon Common was more like skiing than running, but I pushed on and finished in 3:35.

My notes say it was 'tough and muddy but good. I felt strong at the end.' I can't say I felt great the next morning, though. Despite much of the race being off-road, my legs still felt jarred up and I was in no position to run at any speed. I managed a gentle thirty-minute plod on the treadmill, but I didn't know how on earth I would run seven marathons in a row. At this point, it still felt like an impossible dream.

6
Weeks 5-8:
1 October - 28 October 2018

MIKE'S PROGRESS REPORT

Susannah loved the discipline and structure of an elite athlete, working day in and day out on her training. Crucially, she could get herself out of bed on cold, wet dark mornings and go and train.

But she positively comes alive when she races. She becomes a 'running machine'. Focused and determined, she pushes herself and never gives up. Running in races also beats putting in the miles on your own.

We used the races as part of the training schedule. Planning at least one marathon every week gave a good focus to training.

Week 5-8	Monday	Tuesday	Wednesday	Thursday	Friday	Saturday	Sunday	Total running/ walking time
5	**Walk:** 15 minutes **Run:** 45 minutes (easy)	Strength work	**Run:** 15 minutes (warm up) *Intervals:* 20 × 90 second sprints (90 seconds recovery walking after each) **Run:** 10 minutes (cool down) Total running/walking time: 85 minutes	Running School session	**Run:** 40 minutes (easy) *Intervals:* 6 × 1,200m (3 minutes walking after each) **Run:** 10 minutes (cool down) Total running/walking time: 98 minutes (based on 5-minute 1,200m pieces)	**Run for** 90 minutes: 30 minutes (easy), 30 minutes (medium), 30 minutes (marathon pace)	Sussex Marathon: 3:39	552 minutes (9 hours, 12 minutes)
6	**Walk:** 15 minutes **Run:** 45 minutes (easy)	**Run:** 40 minutes (easy) Strength work	**Run:** 20 minutes (warm up) *Intervals:* 20 × 1-minute hill runs (90 seconds recovery walking after each) **Run:** 10 minutes (cool down) Total running time: 80 minutes	Running School session	**Run:** 40 minutes (easy) *Intervals:* 6 × 1,200m (1-minute walking recovery after each) **Run:** 10 minutes (cool down) Total running/walking time: 86 minutes (based on 5-minute 1,200m pieces)	**Run:** 60 minutes (easy)	**Run/walk:** 4 hours. Run 40 minutes (easy) walk 5 minutes (× 4)	566 minutes (9 hours, 26 minutes)

7	**Walk:** 15 minutes **Run:** 60 minutes (easy)	Strength work	**Run:** 20 minutes (warm up) *Intervals:* 8 × 4 minutes (hard) (4 minutes jog recovery after each) **Run:** 10 minutes (cool down) **Total running time:** 94 minutes	Running School session	**Run** for 90 minutes: 30 minutes (easy), 30 minutes (medium), 30 minutes (marathon pace)	**Run** for 90 minutes: 30 minutes (easy), 30 minutes (medium), 30 minutes (marathon pace)	Abingdon Marathon: 3:09	538 minutes (8 hours, 58 minutes)
8	**Walk:** 20 minutes (easy) **Run:** 75 minutes (easy)	Strength work	**Run:** 30 minutes (easy) *Intervals:* 20 × 1-minute runs (90 seconds walking recovery after each) **Run:** 20 minutes (cool down) **Total running/walking Time:** 100 minutes	Running School session	**Run:** 20 minutes (easy) *Intervals:* 20 × 1 minutes (2-minute jog recovery after each) **Run:** 10 minutes (cool down) **Total running/walking time:** 90 minutes	Beachy Head Marathon: 3:52	Wimbledon Half Marathon: 1:34	651 minutes (10 hours, 51 minutes)

Getting into the groove

By the start of October I still lacked confidence, but I was in the swing of following a structured training programme and starting to enjoy it.

Once I say I am going to do something, I really commit to it. This level of determination has its advantages but it also has downsides. Just as I will commit to training, I will also commit to finishing a bar of chocolate, however big it is.

Training was the main focus in my life outside work. I would be thinking about the next training session, recovering from it, and pushing on to the next one. I began to look forward to my weekly sessions at The Running School, even though they were hard work. Each session was like an oasis of stillness where I could focus on my technique.

The sessions were so important for keeping me strong and sound. I could do the long runs by myself, but as the miles added up the flaws in my technique would build and I would end up with sore muscles. My right knee had long stopped hurting after the operation in 2016, but because it had been painful for nearly eighteen months my brain was still trying to tip me away from my right leg on to my left side. My left hip, hamstring and glutes ended up doing more than half the work. Not surprisingly, my left side started to complain in the later stages of long runs.

The sessions at The Running School were broken down into three areas of work depending on my training that week. If I had been racing and had run lots of miles, we would focus on **recovery**. Somewhat bizarrely, this is best achieved by walking backwards on the treadmill. It helps unlock the hips and loosen the muscles and joints, which feels great after a few minutes.

The second focus would be on ensuring I was **moving correctly**. That meant using my hamstrings and glutes, the biggest muscles in my legs, so that they did most of the work when I was running. Before finding The Running School, I had a forward-leaning style; I was dragging myself forward instead of being upright and driving forward from behind. This put all the pressure on my hips, quads and knees, which ached heavily after marathons, while my glutes and hamstrings did almost no work. Mike has hundreds of exercises to work and strengthen the glutes and hamstrings, and a large part of each session was spent doing them. It was tough. My muscles would shake with the shock of being made to work so hard. They really ached after the sessions, and all I wanted to do was lie in a hot bath.

The final focus of most sessions was the **running**. This was always my favourite bit; after all the hard exercises my eyes would light up when I was allowed on the treadmill. I could focus on the tough bits of each session if I knew I'd be allowed to run afterwards.

I would do short bursts on the treadmill, usually no more than twenty or thirty seconds, to make sure my technique was solid. This showed whether I was really engaging my glutes and hamstrings, while being tall through the body and using my arms like pistons to set the rhythm.

Food, glorious fuel

Something odd happened during my second month of training: for the first time in my life, I could not eat enough. As my training increased, Mike kept telling me to make sure I ate enough, but I am not sure I took this seriously at first. I'd lost weight gradually over the past decade because of running, but I was still a healthy weight and I always felt that I ate enough.

Mike's reminders got more frequent. In one session while I was warming up he asked, 'And what do you weigh at the moment?' When I admitted I had lost a couple of pounds, he casually replied that if I couldn't eat enough then we might have to think about protein shakes. He said this knowing I dislike supplements, and much prefer 'real food'.

Without explicitly telling me to get my act together, Mike had made clear that I needed to think more about what, and how much, I was eating. From that moment I made sure that every evening I had a big dinner. It would be a large plate of anything I fancied. Regular dishes included fishcakes with plenty of vegetables (peas, spinach and tomatoes being my favourites), a baguette baked at home with lots of butter, cheese and pickles, or tuna salad. I had a great excuse to eat pizza after long runs. I would also have a proper pudding almost every night. This was usually ice cream with some chocolate or banana bread. Even after all this I would sometimes still be hungry, so I always kept grapes and apples in the fridge.

By November, my weight was stable. Just as I was in a good rhythm with training, so I had found a good balance with nutrition. Thankfully, Mike made no more mention of protein shakes. The daily monitoring helped with this, as there is nowhere to hide when what you're eating is written down in black and white.

Enter the sprint intervals

From week 2 sprint intervals entered the training programme. I love nothing more than disappearing off on a long run, where no one can find me and my mind is clear of all the noise and buzz of modern life. I usually run at a steady pace, working hard but inside my comfort zone.

There is no comfort zone where sprint intervals are concerned. I asked Mike why, when I was running marathons, I needed to do sprint intervals. He said it was to build my heart and lung capacity, improve my ability to run for longer at higher speeds, and make me stronger. I couldn't argue with that.

By week 5 intervals had progressed to fifteen-minute warm-up, followed by twenty 90-second sprints with 90 seconds in between each one. I decided to do these on the treadmill so I could measure my speed and distance accurately. I would then walk for a minute before getting off the treadmill to record my maximum heart rate. Then I'd get back on to do the next one.

It all sounds simple in theory, but it was a strange experience in practice. The session seemed to take forever and by sprints 13 and 14 I was screaming to escape. The sweat poured off me, and my heart rate climbed to 165 beats per minute (not that far off my theoretical maximum of 186 beats per minute). In my notes I added next to interval 17, 'Started to feel sick here as was pushing hard but got through it and felt good at the end.'

I had a great sense of satisfaction afterwards because I had conquered something new. I only had three days until the next intervals session, which was six lots of 1,200-metre pieces. As I would find out in week 7, the toughest session was always eight sets of four-minute pieces. These were short enough to push really hard but long enough to create a lot of lactic acid, which made my legs feel heavy and tired the next day.

From week 5, almost every week involved at least one sprint interval session and I almost started to look forward to them. They are so tough but, a bit like eating broccoli, you know they are doing you a lot of good. I was to find out how much good when I took on my first really big weekend of racing at the end of October.

The breakthrough weekend

It was time to see if the training was having a positive impact on my fitness, endurance and recovery. I did that by racing two days in a row.

I had filled my calendar with a wonderful mix of races. From late October to February is a quiet time for marathons and half marathons, with the best-known races held between spring and autumn. Even so, there were plenty to choose from and sometimes the smaller or more obscure races are the most fun to do. You meet the truly dedicated runners, without the stress of big crowds or the pressure to obtain best times.

For the last weekend of October, I planned to run the Beachy Head Marathon on the Saturday and the Wimbledon Half Marathon on the Sunday. I had run ultras up to 100 miles, so the combined distance of 39.3 miles was well within my limits, but I had never done two races on consecutive days. I knew it was the only way to see how I responded to multi-day racing.

The Saturday was cold, but bright and sunny. The Beachy Head Marathon starts by heading up a steep hill over the cliffs, through woods and lanes, before heading back along the cliffs and down into Eastbourne. I took it at a sensible pace and finished in 3:52. On the drive back to London I refuelled with honey sandwiches, a Toffee Crisp and a big travel mug of tea.

Another new experience now entered my life – the ice bath. Mike had said I must have an ice bath to aid the recovery of my muscles. I ran a cold bath and poured in half a big bag of ice. As a rower at Cambridge and then with the British squad, my younger brother Fred had used ice baths to aid recovery and sleep better at altitude on training camps. When I looked to him for sympathy, there was none. He just told me to get on with it because they really do work.

First, I had to get in. I put my feet in and thought they were going to drop off. I decided that lingering was not going to help and drew on the 'five second rule'. You count backwards from five, and on one you do whatever you need to do. I counted down from five and plunged in on one: wow!

It's a real shock to the system. For about ten seconds, all you can do is think about how unbelievably cold it is. I had to sing out loud to get myself through the teeth-chattering shock of it. Suddenly, you can't feel anything at all. I now take my phone with me so I can distract myself on social media for the ten or twelve minutes I have to stay in: about the time it takes for the ice cubes to melt. Amazingly, my glutes and hamstrings went from feeling really sore to just a little tired.

The next morning, I was up early to run the Wimbledon Half Marathon. I had a good stretch on my exercise mat before leaving the house; everything seemed to be working as it should, and I felt positive. That positivity evaporated as I arrived in Wimbledon and it started to pour with rain. I told myself not to race too hard and to take each mile as it came. Once I got going, I could not believe how good I felt. I was running at almost normal pace. I had a dip in energy between miles 5 and 6, but pushed on and felt good again. Mike said that was probably because I needed to eat a bit more fat the day before to aid recovery. I put that right with a big chocolate Berliner doughnut the following weekend!

I crossed the line in 1:34, which astounded me: I was probably only a couple of minutes slower than I would have expected to be over that course. I wandered home in a happy daze, realising I had made a significant breakthrough over those two days. Mike seemed equally pleased, but he never acts as if anything surprises him. I only came to appreciate afterwards how much thinking, planning and, crucially, worrying Mike did while I just got on with running.

7
Weeks 9–12:
29 October – 25 November 2018

MIKE'S PROGRESS REPORT

With the weather deteriorating quickly in October, we had to increase the workload and the mileage. The plan was to run back-to-back marathons most weekends. Our training included one recovery week for every three 'loaded' weeks. This was not a complete rest, but less volume of training while keeping up the intensity on certain days. The most important block was coming up in December.

Everything was moving along smoothly. Susannah was superb in her training and in her recovery. She approached every training session with the same positive attitude and did not cut corners or complain once. I was impressed.

The only blip we had was her refuelling. Some of the training sessions were making her too tired to eat enough food. This affected her recovery, particularly after the races. With the cold, rain and increased mileage, she was beginning to lose muscle mass, but she ensured that this wasn't a major issue in the end.

Week 9–12	Monday	Tuesday	Wednesday	Thursday	Friday	Saturday	Sunday	Total running/ walking time
9	**Walk:** 15 minutes **Run:** 45 minutes (easy)	Strength work:	**Run:** 15 minutes (warm up) *Intervals:* 20 × 90 second (90 seconds walking recovery after each) **Run:** 10 minutes (cool down) Total running/walking time: 85 minutes	Running School session	**Run for 90 minutes:** 30 minutes (easy), 30 minutes (medium), 30 minutes (marathon pace) Total running time: 90 minutes	Thames Path Marathon: 3:17	Marlow Half Marathon: 1:47	539 minutes (8 hours, 59 minutes)
10	**Walk:** 15 minutes **Run:** 45 minutes (easy)	**Run:** 90 minutes Strength work	**Run:** 20 minutes *Intervals:* 20 × 1-minute hill runs (90 seconds recovery walking after each) **Run:** 10 minutes (cool down) Total running/walking time: 80 minutes	Running School session and physio	**Run:** 40 minutes (easy) *Intervals:* 6 × 1,200m (3 minutes walking recovery after each) **Run:** 10 minutes (cool down) Total running/walking time: 98 minutes (based on 5 minute 1,200m pieces)	**Run:** 3 hours (marathon pace)	**Run:** 4 hours (marathon pace)	658 minutes (10 hours, 58 minutes)

11	**Run:** 90 minutes (easy) **Swim:** 30 minutes (evening)	Strength work	**Run:** 30 minutes (easy) *Intervals:* 8 × 4 minutes (hard) (4 minutes jog recovery after each) **Run:** 10 minutes (cool down) Total running time: 104 minutes	Running School session and physio	**Run** for 90 minutes: 30 minutes (easy), 30 minutes (medium), 30 minutes (marathon pace)	Sunset Marathon: 3:52	**Run** for 90 minutes: 30 minutes (easy), 30 minutes (medium), 30 minutes (marathon pace)	606 minutes (10 hours, 6 minutes)
12	**Walk:** 20 minutes (easy) **Run:** 75 minutes (easy)	**Run:** 40 minutes (easy) Strength work	**Run:** 30 minutes (easy) *Intervals:* 20 × 1-minute hill sprints (90 seconds walking recovery after each) **Run:** 20 minutes (cool down) Total running/walking time: 100 minutes	Rest day	**Run:** 20 minutes (warm up) *Intervals:* 20 × 1 minute (2 minutes recovery jog after each) **Run:** 10 minutes (cool down) Total running time: 90 minutes	**Run:** 13 miles (100 minutes/1:40)	Owler Marathon: 3:37	641 minutes (10 hours, 41 minutes)

Races... and more races

The back-to-back races had gone so well that I wanted to prove to myself it was not a fluke. The first weekend of November was filled with one marathon and one half-marathon. This time it was the Thames Path Marathon on Saturday and the Marlow Half Marathon on Sunday. They both went smoothly, and I finished the marathon in 3:17 and the half in 1:47.

By this stage of the training programme, my mind and body were used to the increased exercise and the higher level of intensity in so many of the sessions. Inevitably aches and pains appeared, but these were mostly where they should be: in my big muscle groups, not in my joints.

Just as I was lucky to be working with Mike, I was grateful to have the support of the entire Running School team. In particular Dahlia Labrenz, a rehabilitation and performance specialist, worked wonders on my legs and shoulders every time they got tight. In just twenty minutes, Dahlia could ensure I walked out of The Running School a lot taller than I walked in. This helped nip any problems in the bud and allowed me to train consistently hard, which I needed to do if I was to get to the World Marathon Challenge.

Running in Shropshire

After two successive weekends of back-to-back races, it was time to hit the hills of Shropshire to get some more miles in the legs. I am incredibly glad that my parents decided to move to Shropshire when I was six and my brother four; it's a beautiful county and an ideal setting for getting fit. It's impossible to run any significant distance in Shropshire without hills. I always feel that 15 hilly miles in Shropshire is worth 20 miles of running on the flat in London, and it's a lot more fun.

I've always been a good sleeper, but with all the exercise I was sleeping like a log. It was typical for me to fall asleep and wake up in exactly the same position. The non-racing weekends gave me a bit more time in bed. I would get up at about 7.45am and be out on the road for 9.30am. If I had three or four hours to run, I could be done by lunchtime.

To take on food and drink without having to carry anything, I planned my long runs as big loops. My favourite running loop was 8 miles, so if I did three loops that would be somewhere between three hours and twenty minutes and three hours and thirty minutes of running. If I needed to run further, to hit the four-hour mark I could do a longer first loop of 11 miles and then two 8-mile loops.

I would leave water, a banana and some Lucozade tablets on the wall outside the back door. Then I could swing into the yard, take what I needed and get back out on the road. It worked well: it ensured that every long run had a structure and a plan to it, while allowing me to stay hydrated and get some nutrition into me. The routes in Shropshire are incredibly varied; although I've run some of my favourite loops hundreds of times, I never get bored of them and love filling my lungs with fresh air.

These long runs by myself were also tough. There was no one to motivate me, other than knowing I would be texting Mike to tell him how it had gone. Also, I never run as fast in training as when I have a number on and I'm racing. I created a mantra, which I learned from reading *The Art of Mental Training*, to get me through the tough moments. My mantra is: 'I'm strong, I'm loving this, push, push!'

Those seven ordinary words were the key to keeping my mind focused on the job in hand. By saying 'I'm strong' I reminded myself of the things I had done to get this far, in both this run and all the runs before. 'I'm loving this' reminded me that no one was making me do this; I was doing it because I love running and I love a challenge – this was my choice. 'Push, push' is what I said to clear my mind of any negativity and send me on my way. Saying all three together always gave me the motivation I needed to keep going.

Everyone will have their own mantra; the important thing is to find out what works for you.

I had still not told my family what I was planning, as I still wasn't confident enough to be open about it. There was some curiosity about why I was running such long distances, but mostly my dad just wondered why I was never back in time for Sunday lunch!

Running in the dark

The following week I practised running in the dark, which I had not done for a long time. The Sunset Marathon near Ironbridge saw competitors run up and down a disused railway line in a 9-mile there-and-back loop. The most interesting thing was that it was to start at sunset – 4.16pm – so I'd be running most of it in the dark with a head torch on.

I had seen on the footage from the 2018 World Marathon Challenge that some of the races took place at night. I had raced through the night before on ultras and enjoyed it. You feel as if you're going faster than you really are, which makes it exciting. You do have to be careful not to trip or fall over.

I had not raced with a head torch for a long time and I'd forgotten how tiring it is when people are running directly towards you and the light is in your face. The miles ticked over nicely that evening and I completed in a sensible 3:52. Like the Thames towpath, the old railway line was far from flat. With it being dark, I didn't want to take the risk of going faster and falling over.

The best bit was getting in the bath (a cold one, followed by a hot one) and then having a big stuffed-crust pizza by the fire before bed. This was a relaxing way to recover. But I made a mistake to learn from. Because it was dark and cool, I didn't sweat much during the race and didn't register that I was thirsty. I had a little water after the race but drank tea with my pizza and then went to bed. I woke up in the middle of the night feeling dehydrated and had to drink two large glasses of water.

Taking a tumble

The next weekend I was back in London and on Sunday I headed for the Owler Marathon near Ashford. This turned out to be more off-road and muddier than I had expected, but I could live with that. What made the race tough was something that had happened forty-eight hours before.

I'd been enjoying a Friday morning leg stretch along the Embankment, wondering what I was going to put on my toast for breakfast, when I caught my toe on a paving stone and went down like a ton of bricks.

I managed to hit my hands and hips but, as usual, my knees took the greatest impact. They looked sore, but I thought I had got away with it. I was only to find that they stiffened up during the day and felt sorry for themselves all of Saturday and into Sunday. There was a bit of heat in them and some inflammation, but there wasn't much I could do about that; only time would heal them.

Mike texted me before the race and asked if I was all right and ready to run. I admitted what had happened on Friday and he said he had thought that something was wrong. A sixth sense is another magical aspect of a good coach. He told me to warm up well and take the early miles gently. I did this and my legs felt very tight for 6 miles, with each stride jarring my knees. Luckily, after that the endorphins kicked in, everything loosened up and I felt pretty much back to normal, finishing in a respectable 3:37.

After bashing my knees so hard, the sensible thing would have been not to race that Sunday. But if I was to fall over in any of the World Marathon Challenge races I would have to carry on – the race wasn't going to be postponed while I recovered. I also hate missing races and wasn't about to start doing so. In the end, I didn't do any long-term harm and by taking part I reminded myself that I am tough and determined, even when things don't go to plan.

8
Weeks 13–16:
26 November – 23 December 2018

MIKE'S PROGRESS REPORT

By now Susannah was running for between ten and twelve hours a week, as well as doing recovery, strength and technique sessions, while having a full-time job! In total this was anything between sixteen and twenty hours a week, with the biggest challenge being the last 'heavy' training block of December.

I needed to give Susannah the belief that she could complete the World Marathon Challenge, even if it meant walking part of it. But I wanted her to 'know' that she could compete and hold her own in the challenge. To do that, we needed to know how far she could push herself.

The four training blocks in December involved running back-to-back marathons every weekend, finishing with running six marathons in just nine days. The plan was to peak at the end of December, reduce the workload for seven to ten days and then build up to peak fitness again for the end of January, when the World Marathon Challenge would begin.

I was nervous and worried. I was confident that Susannah would complete every one of the targets, but at what cost? Would she get injured? Would she get ill?

The month began with marathon-distance runs every weekend and hard interval sessions and speed-endurance sessions during the week. Susannah just got on with it: one day at a time, one session at a time, focused, determined and very tired!

Then we got to the critical sixteen days before Christmas. I was convinced that if Susannah could get through these next two weeks, she would believe that she could get through the World Marathon Challenge.

Our 'nine-day challenge' was different, and, I think, harder. It was much longer and psychologically more intense. Susannah had to do several long runs alone in the cold and wet without anyone else providing food, hydration, logistics or support. She then had to do tough training sessions in between the runs and races.

In the end, all I can say is: wow! What a training performance! I was not at all surprised, but full of admiration for what Susannah had achieved. I don't think Susannah realised until later how well she had performed. This was critical in her preparation. I told Susannah, 'These last two weeks were harder than the challenge: you have nothing to be afraid of.'

Week 13–16	Monday	Tuesday	Wednesday	Thursday	Friday	Saturday	Sunday	Total running/ walking time
13	**Walk:** 15 minutes **Run:** 45 minutes (easy)	Running School session	**Run:** 90 minutes (easy)	**Run:** 60 minutes (medium)	**Run** for 2 hours: 60 minutes (easy), 30 minutes (medium), 30 minutes (marathon pace)	**Run:** 3 hours (marathon pace)	Oulton Park Marathon: 3:39	720 minutes (12 hours, 9 minutes)
14	**Walk:** 20 minutes **Swim:** 45 minutes	**Run:** 90 minutes (easy) Strength work	**Run:** 20 minutes (easy) Intervals: 20 × 1-minute hill runs (90 seconds walking recovery after each) **Run:** 10 minutes (cool down) Total running time: 80 minutes	**Walk:** 30 minutes	Running School session	**Run:** 3 hours (marathon pace)	**Run:** 4 hours (marathon pace)	640 minutes (10 hours, 40 minutes)
15	**Walk:** 20 minutes **Swim:** 45 minutes	Strength work	**Run:** 30 minutes (easy) Intervals: 8 × 4 minutes (hard) (4 minutes jog recovery after each) **Run:** 10 minutes (cool down) Total running time: 104 minutes	Running School session	**Run** for 90 minutes: 30 minutes (easy), 30 minutes (medium), 30 minutes (marathon pace)	Santa's Little Helpers Marathon: 3:23	**Run:** 4 hours (marathon pace)	657minutes (10 hours, 57 minutes)
16	**Walk:** 20 minutes **Swim:** 30 minutes	Enigma Christmas Cracker Marathon 1: 3:35	Enigma Christmas Cracker Marathon 2: 3:28	Running School recovery session	Rest day	**Run:** 4 hours (marathon pace)	12 Days of Christmas Marathon (same course as Santa's Little Helpers): 3:35	898 minutes (14 hours, 58 minutes)

Eat, sleep, run, repeat

By the end of November, I had completely forgotten what it was like not to be on a training programme. The races, the training sessions and the daily monitoring felt like they had always been part of my life. But if I was ever to get complacent, I only needed to run a marathon to remind myself that 26.2 miles is never easy, regardless of how many times you have done it.

December started with the Oulton Park Marathon, which consisted of ten laps of the racetrack. I thought this would be a nice change from running on streets or country roads, and I was looking forward to it. The day before, I had run for three hours, so my legs were not fresh but they were getting used to the back-to-back long weekend runs. What I had not realised until the race began was how tough it is to run on a racetrack designed for cars, not humans. The camber on the bends tipped me on to my inside leg and the short but nasty hill on each circuit was exhausting. It made for a decidedly tough 26.2 miles, and my finish time of 3:37 makes it sound better than I felt.

The next weekend was a non-race weekend, with two long runs in Shropshire: 3 hours on Saturday and 4 hours on Sunday. This solid weekend of training was becoming the norm, but only three months earlier I would barely have been able to do this, let alone consider it a relatively easy weekend.

Planning the big test

Mike said that we needed to simulate the relentless nature of the World Marathon Challenge. This meant putting in a week of running with even more miles and races than I had done before. Although this intimated me, I knew he was right. I wasn't sure how I was going to cope with the travelling, sleep deprivation and unusual eating patterns that would be part of my life as we travelled the 55,000 kilometres around the world, running seven marathons. The only way to see how you will handle multiple races is to have a go at multiple races.

I thought the Christmas period would be a good time to do a few more races. Work tends to quieten down, and I would have a reason to avoid too many parties and drinking opportunities, which were not compatible with training. I had found a couple of marathons around Willen Lake in Milton Keynes that took place on a Tuesday and Wednesday in the middle of December. This would be useful for the mileage and it would be a good mental test to do the same race two days in a row. I also found two more marathons in Kidderminster, near to home, which I could run on the Saturday before and the Sunday after the Milton Keynes races. This gave Mike and I the ingredients needed to plan six marathons in nine days:

- **Saturday 15 December:** The Santa's Little Helpers Marathon near Kidderminster (organised by www.ultrarunningltd.co.uk)

- **Sunday 16 December:** A 'marathon' in Shropshire by myself (three loops of 11, 8 and 8 miles)

- **Tuesday 18 December:** The Enigma Christmas Cracker Marathon 1 in Milton Keynes (organised by www.enigmarunning.co.uk)

- **Wednesday 19 December:** The Enigma Christmas Cracker Marathon 2 in Milton Keynes (organised by www.enigmarunning.co.uk)

- **Saturday 22 December:** A 'marathon' in Shropshire by myself (three loops of 11, 8 and 8 miles)

- **Sunday 23 December:** The 12 Days of Christmas Marathon near Kidderminster (organised by www.ultrarunningltd.co.uk)

This provided a nice balance of four organised races and two 'marathons' by myself. I also liked the symmetry of starting and finishing on the same course in Kidderminster.

Taking on the big test

On the first Saturday, I left London long before it was light. I had my usual pre-race breakfast of Marmite sandwich, a cereal bar, a Rice Krispies Square and a banana. By this stage, I had moved on to decaf tea. I wanted to avoid relying on any food, drinks or stimulants, as I wouldn't be able to count on having them during the World Marathon Challenge.

The weather forecast for the day was awful, with a storm rolling in. I knew it might rain during the World Marathon Challenge, so I just had to get on with it. Soon after the race started, the rain came down heavily and the temperature dropped. A well-known running proverb is 'dress for the second mile', but I like to think 'dress for the fifth mile'. I don't like to put on too many clothes and find myself sweating, losing more precious fluids and salts. By the second half of the race, my gloves were wet and the only way to keep warm was to keep up a good pace.

I crossed the line in 3:23, which was bang on target, but I was freezing cold. The organisers had a tea urn on the go, so I filled my travel mug and hit the road for home, munching on my usual post-race snack of honey sandwiches and a Toffee Crisp. My family was suitably impressed, and after a hot bath followed by roast beef with all the trimmings, I felt great.

The next morning, I felt ready for the second marathon – this time by myself. I don't remember much about the miles but noted 'Legs felt good and tired at 16 miles, didn't seem to deteriorate any more. All the ache in the glutes and hamstrings, none in the quads and knees. Ready to roll for two more in Milton Keynes!' That was as positive as I could hope for.

On the Tuesday morning I was out of bed early and heading up the M1 to Milton Keynes. The glamorous big-city marathons have a great buzz, but there's something special about a low-key weekday race with only thirty-five people. We were all dedicated enough to take a day off work to run ten laps around a lake in Milton Keynes.

The weather was good, and the route was interesting: it weaved clockwise around the lake, passing through a wooded area near the end of each loop. At that end of the course I could hear the traffic from the M1, which reminded me that everyone else was busy in the rat race while I was enjoying a day of fresh air and endorphins. I went off at my usual speed, which I maintained all the way. There was a well-stocked checkpoint on each loop, giving me ten opportunities to refuel. Coming around for the first time, I hastily rammed a whole Jaffa Cake into my mouth and nearly choked. After that, I nibbled them rather than taking them in one.

With a time of 3:35, it was another solid effort and I didn't feel too bad on finishing. The drive back to London was long and boring, but it was good practice for the travelling I'd have to do in the World Marathon

Challenge. Once home, I had an ice bath and ate a filling cheese, potato and onion pie with peas and salad, followed by chocolate yule log and vanilla ice cream. It turns out that training hard in December is an excellent way to enjoy all the best Christmas food! I went to bed feeling tired, not exactly looking forward to the next day but not dreading it either.

After a good night's sleep, I was back on the road to Milton Keynes. This time I knew exactly what to expect, from the race itself to where I was going to park. My glutes and hamstrings were tight though, and I thought it was going to be hard work.

A couple of weeks earlier, Mike had taken me through a warm-up routine to get me moving and ready to race. It started with skipping, something I had not done for a long time. Skipping is a wonderful movement, as it immediately makes you feel lighter on your feet. I incorporated forwards and backwards arm rolls into the skipping, and then skipping crossing my knees over the centre of my body to help loosen off the hips.

Three or four minutes of skipping like this gets your heart going and your body starts to wake up, regardless of how tired or tight your muscles are. After this I did lots of stretching, focusing on my hip flexors, quads, glutes and hamstrings. You can find my full warm up routine at the back of the book.

By the time I was on the start line, I was mentally ready to run. I just hoped my body would hold it together. I got into a lovely rhythm and as I grew in confidence, the laps ticked by. It became clear that I was going to not only complete the fourth marathon, but also do it in a decent time. In the final couple of laps, I pushed to see what was left in my legs. To my surprise, I picked up the speed and finished in 3:28, over seven minutes quicker than the day before. The organisers noticed this, and I joked that I can't have been trying hard enough yesterday. This surprising result was a great confidence boost for marathons 5 and 6 at the weekend.

After four marathons in five days, I knew it was important to look after myself, so I began with another ice bath. But then things went a little off-plan. I glammed myself up, putting on a dress instead of running gear, and headed out for work team Christmas drinks. I was dedicated to my training, but I also believe that you shouldn't miss out on real life. Most of us spend more time with our colleagues than we do with family and friends, and I wanted to be part of the fun. It was a super evening and I was sensible enough to stick to a little prosecco and avoid the espresso martinis. I was in bed by midnight, which I felt was a good running-life balance.

On Thursday I went to The Running School for a recovery session as planned. I then had an easy Friday.

I noted that my calf muscles were tight, but everything else seemed to be in good order. The solo marathon on Saturday was uneventful; my notes say, 'Felt tired to start and had to push through in the middle but felt better after a banana at 19 miles and then finished strongly.' I was now in the zone of being able to run a marathon without having to think much about it.

On Sunday there were even fewer of us running than on the previous Saturday – clearly some people had better things to do on 23 December! I used my new warm-up routine to get moving, feeling keen to get on with marathon 6. I went off at a pace I hoped I could sustain for the whole race. When you get tired, you realise how important your arms are for setting the rhythm: without them working like pistons by your side, your legs will eventually grind to a halt. But if you can set a rhythm with your arms, your legs will follow. We had done a lot of work on this, and with practice I had started to use my arms more efficiently. Now that it really mattered, they were crucial to keeping me going at a solid pace.

When I finished in 3:35, I felt immensely satisfied. Running six marathons in nine days had felt like a huge challenge, but I had done it. I had achieved six race times that were much better than I had dared to hope for, and I was still standing!

The times for each marathon looked like this:

Marathon	Name of Marathon	Distance (miles)	Time
1	Santa's Little Helpers Marathon	26.2	3:23
2	Shropshire run	27	4:02
3	Enigma Christmas Cracker Marathon 1	26.2	3:35
4	Enigma Christmas Cracker Marathon 2	26.2	3:28
5	Shropshire run	27	4:03
6	12 Days of Christmas Marathon	26.2	3:35

I drove home in a happy haze, looking forward to Christmas. We had family staying and I celebrated by drinking far too much champagne. Despite knowing how important good hydration is, I forgot to drink enough water, and I woke up on Christmas Eve with a bit of a headache. Amazingly, my legs felt strong.

9
Weeks 17–21:
24 December – 27 January 2019

MIKE'S PROGRESS REPORT

After a tough six weeks for Susannah, the last week of December was a recovery week. We reduced the volume of running for ten days, but then went back to a couple of high-intensity sessions every week for the next four weeks. Susannah ran another marathon and we planned regular longer-distance runs and interval sessions to keep her focused and sharp. Although we reduced the overall distance covered, we kept the intensity high for five days out of every seven as we moved into the last two weeks.

Susannah was ready.

Week 17–21	Monday	Tuesday	Wednesday	Thursday	Friday	Saturday	Sunday	Total running/walking time
17	Easy day - walking 30 minutes	**Run:** 45 minutes (easy)	**Run:** 60 minutes (steady)	**Walk:** 60 minutes	**Run for 2 hours:** 60 minutes (easy), 30 minutes (medium), 30 minutes (marathon pace)	**Run:** 40 minutes _Intervals:_ 20 × 1-minute hill runs (90 seconds walking recovery after each) **Run:** 10 minutes (cool down) Total running time: 100 minutes	**Run:** 45 minutes (easy)	460 minutes (7 hours, 40 minutes)
18	**Run:** 60 minutes (easy)	New Year's Day Marathon at Dymchurch: 3:38	**Run:** 20 minutes _Intervals:_ 20 × 1-minute hill runs (90 seconds walking recovery after each) **Run:** 10 minutes (cool down) Total running time: 80 minutes	Running School session	**Walk:** 30 minutes	**Run:** 60 minutes _Intervals:_ 20 × 1-minute hill sprints (90 seconds recovery after each) **Run:** 10 minutes (cool down) Total running time: 120 minutes	**Run:** 3 hours (marathon pace)	688 minutes (11 hours, 28 minutes)

								Total
19	**Walk:** 20 minutes **Swim:** 45 minutes	**Run:** 90 minutes (easy) Strength work	Running School session	**Run:** 3 hours (marathon pace)	**Run:** 20 minutes *Intervals:* 20 × 1-minute hill sprints (90 seconds recovery after each) **Run:** 10 minutes (cool down) Total running time: 80 minutes	**Walk:** 30 minutes	**Run:** 4 hours (marathon pace)	640 minutes (10 hours, 40 minutes)
20	**Walk:** 20 minutes **Swim:** 45 minutes	Strength work	**Run:** 30 minutes (easy) *Intervals:* 8 × 4 minutes (hard) (4 minutes walking recovery after each) **Run:** 10 minutes (cool down) Total running time: 104 minutes	Running School session	**Run for 90 minutes:** 30 minutes (easy), 30 minutes (medium), 30 minutes (marathon pace)	**Run:** 60 minutes *Intervals:* 20 × 1-minute hill sprints (90 seconds recovery after each) **Run:** 10 minutes (cool down) Total running time: 120 minutes	Gloucester Marathon: 3:04	518 minutes (8 hours, 38 minutes)
21	Swim or spin class	Running School session	**Run:** 20 minutes (easy) *Intervals:* 20 × 90 seconds (hard) (90 seconds walking recovery after each) **Run:** 10 minutes (cool down) Total running time: 90 minutes	**Run:** 60 minutes (easy)	**Run:** 20 minutes *Intervals:* 8 × 4 minutes on treadmill (4 minutes walking recovery after each) **Run:** 10 minutes (cool down) Total running time: 94 minutes	**Run:** 60 minutes (easy)	**Run:** 2 hours (steady)	424 minutes (7 hours, 4 minutes)

Taking a break... goes wrong

Having trained so hard and got into the pattern of running and racing so often, suddenly I was meant to take a break for a few days. I thought this would be welcome, but I found it odd. Left to my own devices, I managed to injure myself.

I thought I would use the extra time to do some of the exercises Mike had taught me, using resistance bands to engage the glute muscles. I did several sets of exercises for four days in a row. But rather than feeling stronger, I found my legs got tighter and tighter. More worryingly, my lower back started to ache and touching my toes became impossible. Even worse, I had several nights of disturbed sleep as I could not get comfortable with my lower back feeling like it was in spasm. Added to this, I got a cold. My resting heart rate climbed from 47 to 56 beats per minute as my body fought off the bug.

I spent New Year's Eve doing a full kit-list check. I worked out what I was short of and put in an Amazon order for more headbands, socks, shorts and sports bras so I would have seven sets of everything. In Shropshire my sister-in-law, Saskia, had kindly lent me her skiing kit for the marathon in Antarctica. I went into the new year feeling organised, but physically less than great.

On 3 January 2019 I went to The Running School and Dahlia worked her magic on me. By not warming up properly and then over-working my glutes and hamstrings with the bands, I had caused them to pull on my lower back. Dahlia's physio session loosened everything up, and I felt much better.

The final pre-race marathon

It was great to be back into the swing of training, but a nervousness was developing. I had proved I was as ready as I was ever going to be for the World Marathon Challenge, so now it was all about staying in one piece.

The weeks of training followed a similar pattern but were a little lighter as I recovered from the cold and got closer to heading off to Cape Town on 28 January. Rather than doing twenty 90-second sprints on the treadmill, I did twenty 60-second sprints. At weekends I continued to do long runs to keep my legs strong.

I decided to finish on a high: eight days before I was to fly to Cape Town, I ran Gloucester Marathon. The day was cool and clear – ideal winter running weather. Mike told me to simply enjoy it and not to race it. I thought this meant I should aim for 3:20, which would be consistent with my other performances. In the end, I felt so good that I ended up winning it in 3:04. I had come a long way in ten years. This was my fastest race time outside my three best London Marathons, and it took me by surprise. My splits were consistent at 1:32

for each half, which boosted my confidence at just the right time.

Final preparations

With only a week to go before flying to Cape Town, it was time to get organised. I had placed all my kit in a big heap but kept avoiding the rather tedious task of sorting it into piles and checking it would fit into my two bags.

A lot of people taper significantly before a race or competition, but I have never liked that, as it makes me feel lethargic and heavy. Luckily, Mike agreed so I continued to train relatively hard for the final week, which helped to ease the nerves. After my final session at The Running School, it was time to say goodbye to Mike. I told him I wouldn't let him down. He replied that he knew I wouldn't let myself down – it was always about me, never him. We agreed we'd stay in contact and I would text him as needed.

By this stage, the team at World Marathon Challenge had confirmed our numbers. These were based on the alphabetical order of our surnames. I had been allocated number 13, which I rather liked. I like odd numbers but I'm not superstitious, so 13 suited me well and was also memorable. In a twist of fate, this was the same number that Becci Pizzi had been given when she set the female world record for the

World Marathon Challenge in 2016 with an average marathon time of 3:55.

This coincidence led to us messaging each other over Facebook, which was fun and incredibly helpful. Becci's tip about needing good-quality polarised sunglasses proved to be crucial. My full kit list is included at the back of the book.

My final preparations included a pedicure to get my feet smooth and ready to run, a relaxing sports massage and a trip to the cinema to distract me for a couple of hours.

By Sunday I could avoid packing no longer. I laid out all my kit on the floor, putting my running gear for each marathon in a separate labelled zip bag. This ensured that nothing could be forgotten, while giving me a bag for each set of used kit after I ran, so I could keep clean and sweaty kit separate. There was then a host of other items, including four pairs of trainers, cosy clothes for travelling in and a large washbag. Alongside the kit was plenty of food: trusty Toffee Crisps, cereal bars, Marmite and teabags.

With everything packed, I was ready to fly to Cape Town the following night.

PART THREE

COMPETING IN THE WORLD MARATHON CHALLENGE

10
Getting Underway

Heading to Cape Town

The days leading up to my flight were manically busy but also gave me the feeling that time was standing still. It was a relief to be able to zip up my bags and head to the airport for the adventure to begin.

I landed in Cape Town at 7am on Tuesday 29 January. When I got to the hotel my room was not ready, so I left my stuff with reception and went in search of breakfast.

Mike had told me to make sure I did plenty of walking after the flight to wake my legs up, and they certainly needed it. As I wandered along the beach front in the sun, I noticed how heavy and sore my legs felt. I just hoped that they wouldn't feel this way after every flight over the next ten days. I came across Franky's Diner and enjoyed a massive plate of pancakes with maple syrup and butter, which gave me a super energy boost.

At lunchtime I got into my room, had a good stretch and went for a run on the beach front. I was glad to have my factor 50 sun cream: it was hot and, as we were all going to discover, it was only going to get hotter through the week.

After an early dinner, it was time for the pre-race briefing. This was where we'd meet the other runners and collect our numbers and timing chips for each race. When chucked into a new situation with lots of people I tend to be quiet and listen. Here, there was a real buzz with lots of people chatting to each other, some of whom had run other races together and were catching up with old running friends.

The only two runners I knew about were Kristina Schou Madsen and Stéphanie Gicquel. World Marathon Challenge had done profiles of the three of us on social media in the build-up to the event. A professional runner from Denmark, Kristina had done trail races through the jungle and had even represented her country, which was way out of my league. Stéphanie was equally impressive; she was the French twenty-four-hour race champion and had completed a 2,000-mile expedition across the South Pole in seventy-four days, another feat I will never be brave enough to attempt. I didn't think much about the competitive element of the World Marathon Challenge, as I wanted to focus on enjoying the experience. I simply assumed that I would come third.

We each went up to the front to collect our numbers from race organiser Richard Donovan. This had a nice ceremonial feel. I already felt bonded to my number 13 and looked forward to pinning it on to my running vests. We were also given some final details about the event. Each race was specifically organised for us by Richard Donovan, with the assistance of local running clubs and enthusiasts. This was a serious undertaking and included organising the necessary permissions, security and support needed for all the runners. We were going to work to a timetable that would give us 20 hours to complete the final marathon in Miami so we would complete the challenge safely inside the 168 hours available. As well as the forty-one runners, there was a team of between ten and twelve people to look after us. The team consisted of three organisers, a time-keeper, three videographers, two photographers and the team doctor, Dr David Kelly – who we all hoped not to have to bother too much. In addition there would be local teams and first aid support in each location. After the briefing we all felt as informed and as ready to go as we could be.

A final bit of preparation, which was legally required, was to attend a briefing about Antarctica the next morning. The briefing was to be held in central Cape Town at 10am and would be given by The Antarctica Company. Getting there was the perfect way to fit in one last run. It was already hot when I set off after breakfast, so it turned out to be a good rehearsal for the marathon two days later when it was even hotter.

After the busy morning I spent the afternoon relaxing in my room. I meant to sleep, but there was so much to keep updated on that I found myself lying on my bed with my laptop and lots of tea and chocolate, feeling content. World Marathon Challenge were doing regular updates on Facebook and Twitter, so we could already catch up on the briefing from the night before and see all our nervously excited faces.

After signing up to the World Marathon Challenge, I kept it a secret until December. When I made it public, several people asked me who I would be raising money for. It became apparent that it was going to be a wasted opportunity not to support a good cause. I chose SportsAid, a charity I had worked with before which supports Great Britain's next generation of athletes at the start of their careers, arguably when they need it most. It seemed unfair that two people could have equal talent and determination, but only one might get a chance to fulfil their potential because of the circumstances they found themselves in. As someone who is lucky to have had lots of opportunities in life, I wanted to do something positive, however small, for those who do not. The amount raised on my

JustGiving page was growing nicely, and it was fun to thank people for their kind donations.

I headed out for an early dinner, returning to Franky's for a veggie burger and chips, followed by a chocolate sundae. I always think eating vegetables helps minimise the chance of any food poisoning when you're travelling, which is important when you have seven marathons to run.

Afterwards, I laid out my Antarctica kit ready for the morning and turned in for what would be my last night in a bed for nine days. I hoped to get some sleep before the alarm went off at 4am but, as any runner knows, pre-race nerves and excitement can ruin that plan.

Preparing for the 2012 London Marathon and my Guinness World Record attempt. Running shorts went on for the race!

All World Marathon Challenge photographs are courtesy of Mark Colon/World Marathon Challenge.

Winning the 2017 South Downs Marathon in 3:49. Just a shame I fell on my face before the finish

Race 1 in the surreal and wonderful vastness of Antarctica

Race 2 in Cape Town in 30-degree heat

At the end of Race 3 in Perth with Stéphanie (centre) and Kristina (right)

Finishing Race 4 in Dubai and still feeling strong

Kristina and I embrace after a really tough race in Madrid. My fastest marathon of the week, despite being the fifth one!

Heading off into the night at the start of Race 6 in Santiago

Gathered together on the start line in Miami for our final race

With the men's winner and World Record Holder Michael Wardian: a moment I never thought could happen to me

Running Manchester Marathon in April 2019 in a new best time of 2:56

With Mike at The Running School with the World Marathon Challenge Trophy

11
Novo, Antarctica: Getting Going

> **TEXTS BEFORE ANTARCTICA**
>
> Hi Mike, all well here! The briefings are done and we're off to Antarctica! Legs were heavy when I arrived on Tuesday but moved around lots, slept and eaten plenty so ready to go. Will keep you updated!! S

Setting off for Antarctica

When the alarm went off, I was relieved to find I had got some sleep, albeit with some vivid dreams. I had a shower and a cup of tea before meeting everyone downstairs ready to get the coach to the airport at 5am. The hum of conversation from downstairs created a buzz of excitement. I remember wondering how long this would last into the week once energy levels dropped. My room was booked through to the Friday, so I only had to take what I needed for Antarctica – but even that filled my smaller bag.

At the airport I bought the latest Jack Reacher book, *Past Tense*, which I would dip into between naps over the next five days. Our plane for Antarctica was seriously cool. Overall, I am non-plussed by celebrity and extravagance, but this plane was the luxurious flying machine used by U2 and Bill Clinton when they travelled the globe. It certainly gave me a glimpse of how the other half live.

We had a lovely team looking after us on the plane, and I enjoyed a breakfast of fruit, granola and yogurt followed by a veggie cooked breakfast and a bread roll with peanut butter. The food on the plane was good throughout the World Marathon Challenge, but the portions were smaller than we were used to. We all had to top up with things we had brought with us, which in my case was plenty of Cadbury's chocolate, Toffee Crisps, Rice Krispies Squares and Eat Natural cereal bars, as well as the nuts, crisps and fruit which were available on each flight. Some runners had brought pots of noodles and other food that could be rehydrated; anything that has been 'cooked' is always comforting.

We had all been allocated seats, and I found myself next to Kristina. We'd had a short chat at the Antarctica briefing but it was good to talk more. Of course, she had perfect English to my zero Danish, as is so often the British way. The flight was smooth, and we all dozed a bit once we'd eaten. I was continuing to keep my diary so made notes in it during the flight. I noticed Kristina also had one. We were obviously both organised people who liked to plan and reflect on things.

Hello, beautiful Antarctica

The first glimpse of Antarctica was one of those special moments in life. It's so unbelievably beautiful. All you can do is describe it as very white, but that doesn't do it any form of justice. It's so clean and pure: everything a noisy and busy city like London is not.

Antarctica is a desert twice the size of Australia, and surprisingly, it rarely snows. On stepping off the plane it's the sheer brightness that hits you. Without a good pair of polarised sunglasses you would rapidly go snow-blind. The plane had stopped 250 metres away from a series of huts, each with a different purpose. The women were given one hut to change in; the men had two, as there were more of them. Further down the row was a food hut, which acted as the canteen for the Russian and US workers based there, and the all-important bathroom hut, which was painted in zebra colours.

We had about an hour before the race, so I ate a bar of chocolate and wandered over to see where we would be running. The circuit was a big oval where the snow had been slightly compressed, marked out with small blue flags.

Trying a short run, I was surprised by how hard it was to move across the snow. We had been told we didn't need spikes, as ordinary trail trainers would be suitable, so I might have been lulled into a false sense of security. In fact, the whole course would turn out to vary rather a lot, with some mushy bits, icy patches and a crosswind that would get stronger throughout the afternoon.

For now, all I could do was get ready to race. I went through my tried and tested warm-up routine. Mike and I had discussed this routine on several occasions, and it proved vital for me. Throughout the week I was surprised by how little anyone else warmed up before we began running. I found that doing my routine before every marathon ensured I was physically and mentally ready to race.

Back in the women's hut, we were calm and focused. I am sure we were all wondering quite how we had found ourselves in Antarctica, about to run one of only two marathons held there every year. The other is the Antarctic Ice Marathon, which Richard Donovan organises each December. Other marathons in the area are hosted on George Island; to purists, this does not count as Antarctica because it's not connected to the mainland.

Once in running kit, we all made a trip to the bathroom hut at some point. There isn't much water, so the toilets have a clever system of plastic bags that seal when you 'flush'. Back at the start, there were a couple of tents and a food table, which would act as the checkpoint on each loop. Things weren't quite ready and as we milled around I found I had to do a last-minute dash to the bathroom hut, which at least provided more practice for running on the snow.

Finally, we got together for the pre-race briefing and a numbers check. Each of us had to say 'yes' when our number was called out to make sure no one was missing. We were told we would be going anti-clockwise, first going out to do a half loop and back, and then doing six full loops. The GPS trackers would show that we ended up running 44.3 kilometres, as opposed to 42.2 kilometres, but I'd rather go further than come up short!

Before we could get going properly, we had to do a 'false start' for the cameras. In a real start, so many people are busy setting their watches that it looks hopeless as a photograph. I made sure to run as little as possible and get back into a good position for the real start.

The race

Finally, the horn went off and the official 168-hour clock started. The World Marathon Challenge was on! We quickly spread out as we found our pace. I tried to set off at a decent speed and find a rhythm I could maintain, but I soon realised this was going to be tough. My feet were moving about a lot and it was hard work just to maintain a fairly ordinary pace.

At first Kristina and I were about level, with Stéphanie just behind, but by the time we had done the out-and-back and set out on the first full loop it was clear that Kristina could maintain a better pace than me. I just settled in for the miles ahead. This was the one race in which I did not listen to music: I wanted to simply appreciate the experience and enjoy running in Antarctica, as I didn't think I'd have the chance to come back.

On coming into the checkpoint after the first full lap, I found to my frustration that none of the drinks had been poured out. I might be behind Kristina, but I didn't want to lose ground unnecessarily. I immediately apologised for being grumpy while I had an orange energy drink and an Oreo cookie.

I felt better once the first lap was done. I consciously told myself to stop fighting the snow, accept this was going to be hard work and enjoy it. At the furthest end of each loop, I could really appreciate the vastness of Antarctica. In the middle of the race I had the crazy endorphin-fuelled thought of running off the course into the middle of nowhere. Would anyone notice? How long could I survive for? I decided against finding out the answer to these questions.

By now I was familiar enough with the course to know which bits I rather liked and which were really tough. On the lower side there was a bit more ice, which made it slightly easier; along the top side we were in the wind and the snow was more uneven. As our feet chopped it up, it got deeper and tougher to run in. Getting to the end of each circuit and having an Oreo cookie with an energy drink and water became something I really looked forward to.

On my penultimate loop I was lapped by Michael Wardian, the leading male runner. Michael was running the World Marathon Challenge for the second time, having set the world record with an incredible average marathon time of 2:45:57 in 2017. Michael is an amazing runner and, as I was to learn, an awesome guy. He lives in Arlington in the US and has a proper job, but he races regularly all over the world. He's just the kind of person you would want to share a trip like this with, as he was encouraging and positive throughout.

By this stage Michael was down to just shorts, which was impressive. I had ditched my gloves and worn a headband rather than a hat, so heat could escape from my hands and head. With a Buff around my neck to keep my nose warm when the wind got up, I was just the right temperature throughout the race.

In the final half circuit I tried to pick the pace up a little, but this was difficult in the snow. I was determined to finish in under four hours and had worked out I was safely on course for that if nothing went wrong. I crossed the line in 3:53:33, which I was satisfied with. As Richard put a medal around my neck, I muttered something like 'Wow, that was hard work, I'm never running on snow again.' But with the endorphins flowing, those of us finishing chatted about how great it all was. Kristina had loved the run, as was to be expected given her trail experience. I was just glad to have completed the first marathon safely.

A cheerful evening

Every runner is allowed eight hours to complete each marathon during the World Marathon Challenge, so we would not be leaving Antarctica for some time. There was no great hurry to do anything or be anywhere.

I headed back to our hut and had a good stretch, pleased to find that nothing seemed too tired or sore. Making use of the tiny amount of water available, I washed my face and neck and then put on some warm, dry clothes. I should have packed a second pair of trainers, as inevitably mine were damp. With some dry socks on, I made my way to the food hut to see what was on offer, carrying my diary for making post-race notes.

The food hut was cosy and warm, with about six long tables and twenty chairs set out in front of an old-school canteen. This was managed by two burly Russians cooking up big pots of food for the people who lived at the airbase. As I always do after a race, I reached for the first of what would be half a dozen cups of tea during the evening. Avoiding the soup because I couldn't tell what was in it, I had some peanut butter sandwiches on white bread – a reliable way to refuel.

Only a few of us had finished by this stage, so I got on with writing my post-race diary. By 7.30pm most of the Russians and Americans had left and the place was ours. We were told that there were some sausages and mashed potato for us. I ducked the sausages but devoured a plate of mash with tomato ketchup swirled through it. Because of limited supplies in Antarctica there weren't any fruits or vegetables to eat, but there were plenty of Mars bars so I was happy enough.

As more people finished, we began comparing experiences. Most people were in good shape, just relieved to have completed the marathon in one piece and be out of the cold and the wind, which had increased throughout the race. A couple of runners did not feel great and Dr Kelly was kept busy for a while, making sure everyone was rehydrating properly and getting warm.

One of the many wonderful things about the World Marathon Challenge is the mix of people it brings together. As the hut door opened and another runner entered with an exhausted but happy grin on their face, it was clear that we were already starting to bond over this shared experience. Several people had come as couples or in small groups, and their in-jokes and shared experiences made it fun for us all. People would peel off to go back to their hut for some more warm clothes or a lie down. I stayed in the hut; it was cheerful and warm, and it was relaxing to sit and chat and write my diary.

One of the last people to come in was seventy-six-year-old Dan, who had completed the marathon in 7:11. I can't imagine how brutal it must have been to be out in the cold for that long; I had massive admiration for him. Despite being freezing, he made no fuss; he just helped himself to some cereal, as all the hot food had disappeared. I'd been going through my rucksack to tidy it up and came across my hand- and foot-warmers, which I'd completely forgotten I'd packed. I stuck two in each shoe and immediately felt my feet warm up. I had some spare hand-warmers, so I gave a couple to Dan, who was still shaking with cold.

During the week I was to find out that lending and borrowing bits of kit, big or small, came in handy. Any small act of kindness was always repaid; as we all know, this is how the world goes round.

At about 10.30pm the word went out that we would be leaving at midnight. We headed back to our huts to relax for a bit. People had different approaches to recovery; some curled up on the bunk beds, while others used equipment on their muscles. Several people had NormaTec Pulse recovery machines, which inflate and send pulses down the legs, helping the muscles to relax and recover. They were to become a regular sight on the plane.

We were all ready for some sleep by the time we boarded the plane. Despite it being late at night, it was still bright as we all wandered across the ice for the last time. I looked over at the race circuit, which still had the little blue flags marking it out. It looked lonely without all of us bringing it to life. I couldn't imagine that the residents of the Novo airbase were going to make any further use of it: even though I love running, if my only option was to run on snow and ice then my mileage would drop rapidly.

We had only been on Antarctica for twelve hours, but it felt like a lot longer. We'd all enjoyed a unique and special experience, but now it was time to think about the next race, which was only a few hours away. Despite eating earlier, I felt ravenous and devoured my aeroplane veggie breakfast and a chocolate protein bar before pulling up my blanket and nodding off. I had only about three and a half hours' sleep, but I didn't feel tired. I felt ready for the second race.

In each chapter in this section I have shared an excerpt from my marathon diary. In my diary, I summarised the positive and negatives to take from the marathon I had just completed. This snapshot reminded me what had gone well and what I needed to prevent becoming an issue in the next race. It was a useful way of closing my thoughts on what I had just done and moving on to the next chapter with a fresh and positive outlook. As Mike had said, it was just a case of one race at a time.

What follows are the exact notes I made after the Antarctica marathon.

RACE SUMMARY: ANTARCTICA

Positives

- Heart rate and lungs good – heart rate at 150 [beats per minute], then down to 145 for the second half.
- Legs ache in the right places – all in the glutes/ hamstrings, not in the knees and quads.
- Think I am running level – left and right legs feel equal.
- Nutrition was good – water, Powerade, Oreos worked well.
- Shoe selection – about right. Probably didn't need size 7½, could have used 7.
- Got kit right – light layers were spot on. Bandana was helpful for runny nose.

Negatives

- I did NOT like running on snow – I am too big and lumpy to run on uneven snow – hard work.

- I was one-paced – completely – but hopefully that was the snow, and I can be back to speed on the pavement tomorrow.

- Hamstrings are tight – need to keep stretching them now – got my feet up on a chair stretching my hamstrings so should help.

- NB Must warm up very well tomorrow for Cape Town Marathon.

12

Cape Town, South Africa (Africa): Into My Stride

Welcome back to Cape Town

We landed at about 6.30am and boarded a bus back to the hotel. We then had to sit in near stationary rush-hour traffic as the day outside got hotter and hotter. I sat next to Michael – or 'fast Mike', as I called him in my diary – and we chatted away. I knew I needed to eat something but would not have time for a proper breakfast, so I settled on an Eat Natural cereal bar and a Rice Krispies Square.

Richard said we were to get back to the hotel, change and be ready to race as quickly as possible. There wouldn't be enough time to shower, given that the aim was to get the race underway by 8.15am. But I decided I just had to have a quick shower to wash off the dried sweat so my sun cream would soak in – it was definitely going to be a day for sun cream.

After cleaning my teeth and enjoying a quick shower I felt cooler and ready to go. I applied two layers of sun cream and put on my running kit. This consisted of a thick Gore headband to stop sweat running into my eyes, sunglasses, a Nike sports bra, my favourite pink running vest (which read SUZE across the front and had a lot of pin holes from race numbers over the years), black Ron Hill running shorts (which are nice and long and high-waisted so sit comfortably), thick Hilly Twin Skin running socks and size 7 men's Asics. I'd been wearing men's shoes for several years, since someone pointed out how much sturdier and better made they are than the women's version.

This time I popped my MP3 player into my back pocket, along with a lip balm. I also like to have a couple of pieces of kitchen roll tucked into my waistband, as I always get a runny nose in the early miles. I ended up leaving it in the hotel bathroom at the last minute, but I coped just fine: this goes to show that we don't always need the little things we become fixated on.

We gathered outside the hotel, everyone stretching and trying to stay in the shade as the temperature continued to rise. Richard told us we were to start on the pavement across from the hotel, head down the beach front, loop back up past the hotel and then back again, completing 10-kilometre loops and then another 2 kilometres to make up the full marathon distance.

In the main checkpoint in the middle of each loop there would be water, energy drinks and snacks; at either end there would be water in the form of small plastic cubes you break with your teeth. At this point Dr Kelly stepped in to say he wanted to see us all stopping to take on a proper amount of fluid at the checkpoint, not just chucking the water on our faces. He reminded us that last year's competitors had got very dehydrated and it was hotter this year. We were all just itching to get going.

The race

The race finally started at 8.53am, and off we headed down the main beach front road. If you were a local person or a visiting tourist, you would surely have wondered what was going on.

It was a relief to find that my legs did not feel too bad at all. Most importantly, it was a joy to be back on tarmac, which was firm and consistent underfoot in comparison to the snow. I focused on trying to get into a nice rhythm without thinking about the 26 miles ahead.

I was slightly in front of Kristina as we approached the first turnaround point, but too far behind Michael to see exactly where we would be turning. The course was marked out by members of a local running club holding red flags, so I assumed it would be obvious. As we all know, it's best never to assume things in life.

Somehow, I ended up running about 20 metres past the small roundabout that was the turnaround point. The road immediately rose up a steep hill, so I knew I should have turned. I looked around and saw one of the volunteers with their flag and other runners heading back along the beach front. I cursed under my breath at my stupid mistake but tried not to waste energy by being annoyed.

Kristina was now about 30 metres ahead of me and running well. When we talked about this afterwards, Kristina said she'd shouted at me when I'd missed the turnaround point but I hadn't heard, and I believe her. We had good competition all week, but it was fair competition and we all genuinely tried to help each other.

I made it my mission to work my way back to Kristina and overtake her. In hindsight, having her as a target for the next few kilometres gave me a focus and settled me into a strong rhythm. After the second turnaround point at 8 kilometres, I eventually overtook her. I put on a little push to ensure there were some clear metres between us, as I wanted some space to run without racing another competitor.

It was now most definitely hot. I was sweating, but I felt under control. I am fair and burn easily, but as long as I have factor 50 sun cream on and keep hydrated, I cope well with running in the heat. I reminded myself that I'd run in Egypt and other hot places and always coped, so this would be no different. The miles ticked away nicely through the middle section of the race. At this stage it was sinking in that I was really running the World Marathon Challenge and my long-held ambition was becoming a reality. It's a privilege to be able to run marathons, especially in wonderful places like Cape Town, and I always keep that front and centre of my mind when I start to get tired.

I made sure to heed Dr Kelly's advice and take on board as much water as I could, along with energy drinks and sweets at the main checkpoint. In the end we all did a good job keeping hydrated, but some people did less well on applying sun cream, going by the post-race tan lines.

As with the vast majority of the marathons I have run, this race fell into three distinct phases. They always look something like this:

Phase 1: This is normally between the start and mile 7 or 8. I get going and my brain is racing, probably faster than my legs. Life seems to whizz through my mind – things I need to remember to do, TV programmes I've watched, books I've read and conversations I've had. With all this going on there's limited time to think about how fast I am running, but these are usually my quickest miles so I'm in a good rhythm for the middle part of the race.

Phase 2: At some point, normally about mile 8 or 9, or a little over an hour in, my brain switches off. The endorphins take over, the fast thinking slows down, and I just enjoy running. If things are going well, I am in a strong rhythm and every part of my body is swinging along smoothly. I always hope this phase will last forever. Sadly, this is always just a dream.

Phase 3: Between 16 and 21 miles there comes a moment when I realise over the course of around a hundred paces that it hurts. Every stride hurts. The glutes ache a little, the hamstrings tighten, and I know I will be working hard all the way home to maintain stride length and pace. On the best days this moment doesn't arrive until after 19 or 20 miles, but on the tougher days it's there at mile 16, which makes it a long 10 miles home. Whenever it arrives, it's time to dig in.

Cape Town followed this pattern exactly and as I began the final loop with 12 kilometres (just over 7 miles) to go, I suddenly felt tired. My legs still felt relatively good, but I felt drained because of the heat. I started to get salt forming on my face from the drying sweat, and no amount of fluid I could take on during the race would stop me feeling dehydrated. But I also knew I only had 12 kilometres to go.

The useful thing about being on a course with turn-around points at the end of each loop is that you get a chance to run back towards your fellow competitors. This allows you to check two vital things. First, what's the distance between you and the next runner? Second, how does the other runner look? Is their stride still consistent and their head up, or are they looking tired? I always try and look as strong as possible as I head back towards them, however little I might be feeling like that.

Once I was ahead of Kristina, I was able to use the turnaround points to validate that distance between us. It grew throughout the race, which was a confidence boost. Not far behind Kristina was the French runner Stéphanie. Every time I saw her running, I was blown away by how good she looked. She has an incredibly long and elegant stride, and just makes running look easy. I could not quite understand how I was moving faster than her, but I was and that's all that mattered.

Once inside the final few kilometres I was ready for the race to be over. I needed to get out of the sun, have a shower and refuel. I had started to dream of a burger and fries from Franky's Diner, which motivated me to get to the line as quickly as possible.

I wasn't quite sure what we were meant to do for the final 2-kilometre section and started to worry at the final turnaround point that I would take the wrong course. Clearly, the organisers were not going to let us take the wrong route, but when you're tired and wanting the line to come, the small things start to play on your mind. This was especially relevant given that I'd already made the early mistake which had seen Kristina come past me.

As I ran back to towards the hotel, where the final 2-kilometre section was to begin, I shouted to a fellow runner that I didn't know where to go. This turned out to be Stéphanie's husband, Jérémie Gicquel, who was competing in the half marathon and had finished. He pointed down the coast and indicated to just keep going and someone would send me back towards the finish. Feeling a bit calmer, I kept running as fast as my legs could take me. Right on cue, another kilometre further down the road, one of the race organisers pointed back towards the finish and I made the final turn for home with just one more kilometre to go.

I always try to enjoy the last section of a marathon, because every race is special. If you've had a tough race and haven't run as well as you would like, it's a relief to be getting to the line. If you're on target or running faster than you planned, then the final section feels immensely satisfying. On this occasion, although I was undoubtedly tired, it felt good. I was in a beautiful setting and about to *win* a World Marathon Challenge race.

As I approached the line with the tape out in front of me, it was wonderful to put my arms in the air and even better to stop running. I was satisfied with my time of 3:21:32, but there are no celebrations when you're only on race 2 of a seven-race competition. My priority was to get out of the sun as quickly as possible. I went over to the refreshments area, which was under a gazebo, and drank plenty of water. I never feel like eating when I finish a marathon, but chilled water always tastes amazing.

The organisers asked me to pose for some pictures and give a short interview, which I happily did. I love talking about running and when you're on a cloud of endorphins the words come even more easily.

Just over three minutes after I had finished, Kristina crossed the line. We agreed we were both relieved to have finished and could start the process of preparing ourselves ready for our third race. Stéphanie was only another twelve minutes behind Kristina and was still running well.

I headed back to the hotel for a shower and was pleased to find that the aching was evenly spread. Crucially, both legs felt equally sore, so I was clearly using them as a pair. My right knee was not causing me any issues, which was always a worry in the back of my mind. This would end up affecting me in the sixth and seventh races, but they were a long way off for now.

Post-race refuelling

Once clean, it was most definitely time for food. I had some postcards and my diary to write so headed off up to the next street to Franky's ready to write and eat. I sat in the cool of the diner and had a delicious veggie burger with fries, coleslaw and onion rings, adding plenty of salt, tomato ketchup and mayonnaise. I followed it up with an enormous chocolate milkshake, which was almost pure ice cream. I felt absolutely stuffed as I wandered back to the hotel.

On arriving back, I found the bus outside with a few fellow runners getting on. This was the first run to the airport; there would then be a second one for later finishers. I wanted to get to the airport early, so I whizzed upstairs (as fast as I could manage after two marathons well inside twenty-four hours), packed, checked out and gave my stamped postcards to Reception to send on.

The traffic was heavy and it took over an hour to get to the airport. As the bus would be going back to the hotel and returning in the early evening rush-hour traffic, it was clear we'd have time to kill at the airport. Others talked about needing to get some sleep, but I didn't feel tired despite knowing I must be. The endorphins were overriding fatigue for the moment.

For the rest of the trip we would be on a chartered Titian Airways plane. This was to become our home in the air as we flew to Perth, Dubai, Madrid, Santiago and eventually Miami. Several runners got on the plane straight away to sleep, but I felt I was going to be spending enough time on it so I decided to check my emails in the airport.

Running is the central aspect of the World Marathon Challenge but making sure you recover as effectively as possible is an important secondary factor. There's no point being in a hurry or getting annoyed about the travelling. It's all about making the most of the full 168 hours you have to complete the challenge. When I got on the plane at Cape Town, I felt I was starting to understand that.

When asked if I had a seating preference, I had said I'd like a quiet seat. My idea of hell would be to sit next to someone who wanted to talk all the way around the world. We all react differently to big challenges and nerves. Some people become extroverts and can't stop talking, while others become quiet and almost mono-syllabic. I am in the second category; I keep myself to myself when I'm in unusual circumstances. I was therefore delighted to be allocated a double seat, 41A and 41B, as my home for the next five days.

I don't know if the organisers did this deliberately, but they put Kristina and me opposite each other with Stéphanie and her husband just behind. It was already clear that one of us would win the 2019 World Marathon Challenge, but we got on well and there was a healthy competitive spirit between us. This was lucky, as there could have been a rather tense atmosphere otherwise.

As it was, I kicked off my trainers and socks, put on the complementary travel slippers and settled back into my comfy seat for some much-needed sleep.

RACE SUMMARY: CAPE TOWN

Positives

- I won. Let's be honest, that matters.
- Good to be back on road. Oh, what a joy all the races are on a hard surface now.
- Legs were solid - less hamstring ache afterwards.
- Eating and drinking is going well.
- Still looking forward to the next race!

Negatives

- Worked hard in the sun - heart rate high at 170 [beats per minute]. Not sure it should sit that high.
- Got tired in the last 12 kilometres. Was this the pace or the heat? Will find out in No. 3.
- Small blister on left foot - hopefully not an issue, let's see.
- Must warm up well - cannot do too much!!

TEXTS AFTER CAPE TOWN MARATHON

Hey Susannah well done for both
[marathons] very happy for you, how are
you feeling?

> Hi Mike, today was hot!! But legs feel good
> and off for a burger and chips as need some
> salt back in me. Warm-ups are working a
> treat! Got 18 hours until Perth. Some people
> are a lot less well prepared!! S

Well done eat and recover well. We know
that you are very well prepared! And will get
stronger. Follow your routines we know they
work. Text me when you can, good luck with
Perth – another hot one. Mike

13
Perth, Australia (Oceania): Cruising Along

Up, up and away

The journey to Perth consisted of three flights, with refuelling stops at Mauritius and Jakarta. At the start of the week I'd thought it would be tedious to keep going through the landing process: folding away trays and putting on seat belts would disturb rest and recovery. But I quickly realised I was never going to sleep for more than three or four hours at time.

My seat tipped well back, but it was not a flat bed so getting my legs into a comfortable position could be difficult. Several times during the week, I woke with such heavy legs that my quad muscles felt as if they were about to cramp. This was a combination of lactic acid in the muscles and the feeling of heavy legs that we all get when we fly long distances.

The only way to deal with this was to get up and move about, so I spent plenty of time walking up and down the aisle. I also enjoyed lying on the floor with my legs up against the wall, which drained the blood out of my feet and stretched the back of my legs. Kristina lent me her foam roller, which did wonders for my tight glutes and hamstrings. This proved vital to keeping me sound, and I wonder how I would have felt if Kristina had not been so generous.

I also became hungry every three or four hours. I have never been able to sleep through hunger and this was not the time to start trying, so I ate plenty of the peanuts, fruit and snack bars that were on offer between meals. By the time we landed in Perth I had got into the swing of living on a plane. That was a relief, as there was a lot more flying to do – but first it was time for the next marathon.

An awesome Aussie welcome

We were due to land in Perth at 6.45pm local time and start running at 8.30pm. Because our fuel stops had taken longer than expected, it was approaching 9pm as we headed out through Arrivals to a warm welcome from our Australian hosts, which (of course) included a large inflatable kangaroo. The organisers could not have been more friendly and helpful, and we were all in good spirits after plenty of rest on the plane.

We were taken by bus to the running club at the Burswood Water Centre, which is next to the Swan River a couple of kilometres away from Perth Stadium. On the bus I tried to take in Perth and my first experience of Australia. I knew my legs were tired, but I was still looking forward to running and felt surprisingly calm and focused.

Everything was perfectly set up for us at the running club. We had a big room to get ready in and a dozen inflatable mattresses for anyone wanting a rest after running. Tables, chairs and food were set out in a room next door. We were also told there were showers somewhere but we weren't ready to think about that yet: first we needed to run the marathon.

It was night-time and some people were getting their head torches out, so I did the same. Inevitably, my head torch, which I had worn before and was fully charged when I left the UK, refused to turn on. Cue a mini panic before Kevin Cochrane, a runner from the US, came to my rescue with a charging pack and a spare head torch. This was another example of how kind everyone was to each other. As I was getting ready, a consensus emerged that we would not need head torches after all, as the route was lit all the way. I left mine charging just in case and went to warm up.

Outside the running club there was a long trestle table with water, energy drinks, sweets and snacks. Volunteers were buzzing about checking everything was ready for us. I jogged off in need of a few quiet minutes and a good stretch. I was concerned by how heavy my legs felt and especially how tight my hamstrings still were. I felt as if I was moving like an enormous crab, with every joint unable to straighten fully. This was hardly a surprise, given that I'd run two marathons in the last forty-eight hours. I went through all the warm-up stages that Mike and I had discussed, starting with skipping and moving on to all the stretches. Slowly, my body started to feel better. I had to stretch every muscle group several times, but fifteen minutes later I jogged back to the club house moving more freely and feeling ready to go.

The race

I grabbed my MP3 player and, after a final bathroom stop, went out to the start line where everyone was gathering. Richard briefed us that this was a twelve-loop course. We would be running up to Perth Stadium, turning around and coming back past the start, before turning again and running back to complete a loop. A multi-loop course like this sounds mentally taxing because it's so repetitive, but it also has lots of advantages. It means more opportunities to refuel and rehydrate at the drinks table, and plenty of opportunities to check where you are in relation to other competitors. Crucially, the track was on tarmac and completely flat, which I knew would suit me.

The starting horn went at 11.45pm. As was becoming the usual pattern, Stéphanie, Kristina and I started off side by side. I didn't want to be racing them both so I pushed on ahead into a bit of space, taking my usual position behind the leading men. It felt good to know that my legs were working as they should. It had been hot during the day, but the night temperature was ideal for running. The only irritation throughout the race was the water sprinklers for the grass, which spent most of the time watering the tarmac we were running on. I hate having wet feet so I did my best to avoid them, but on the final turn for home one of them soaked me.

My aim was to get into a solid rhythm and stay in it for the whole race. As we made the first turn and ran back towards the start/finish area, I was nicely tucked in behind the leading men. I don't know if I admitted this to myself at the time, but I must have been worried about where Kristina and Stéphanie were, as I decided I needed to go faster. As we went through the finish/start area I picked up the speed and tried to push on. In hindsight, this was a bad decision: I should have simply stuck behind the the leading men and used their rhythm and energy to pull me along. When we all discussed this, I agreed it wasn't the best in-race decision I had ever made.

I completed the first loop in just under sixteen minutes. Allowing for a bit of slowing down throughout the race, this put me on track for a 3:15 to 3:20 marathon, which was spot on. At the second turnaround point, I was able to calculate the distance between me, Kristina and Stéphanie. Kristina was closest behind at first, but during the course of the race Stéphanie overtook her and was never far behind me. She still seemed to be running so smoothly and, while I was in control of the situation, I didn't feel I could relax for a single mile.

As I always do, I played games in my head. I broke the loops up into the first quarter of the race (three loops), then the first third (four loops), then pushing on for halfway (six loops), then three-quarters (nine loops) and so on. Doing the smallest calculations becomes entertainingly difficult when all your energy is going into your legs; there's little left for your brain to operate on.

I grabbed water, energy drinks and one or two chewy sweets on every lap to keep fuelled. My legs got better and better throughout the race. At some point, my hamstrings gave up arguing and I could move much more freely. Inevitably I got tired towards the end, but this was overtaken by my internal jubilation about being close to winning my second race. The miles were effortlessly ticking by and in each lap I was stretching my lead by a few metres over Stéphanie, who was comfortably ahead of Kristina. On the final turn, after the drenching from the water sprinkler, I pushed for home and crossed the line in 3:19:19 – bang on my early target.

As I was crossing the line and taking the ribbon, Stéphanie was passing through in the other direction. She finished only four minutes behind me in 3:23:45, followed closely by Kristina in 3:24:46. We were given our medals and the photographers took a great picture of us. It was going to be an ultra-competitive week, but we would make sure we enjoyed it together.

Firing up the barbecue

I headed back to the club house for a really good stretch. Kristina was there too, and we joked about the state of our legs while connecting on Facebook. She sent the picture of the three of us to me on AirDrop. Despite the tiredness, my legs felt better than they had before the race. My body was starting to accept that it needed to do what I was telling it to do.

One of the volunteers showed us to some spacious showers at the back of the club. We had not been told to bring towels, but I had packed a small one just in case. Kristina didn't have one and I was pleased to be able to return the foam-roller favour and lend her mine. When you've run a marathon and need a shower, you aren't going to be squeamish about sharing a towel.

I took care to scrub my feet well to get all the sweat and dirt off before moisturising and putting on some thick socks so the skin could start to recover. After ten years of marathon running, I don't get the blisters you typically see on newer runners' feet anymore, but I have pressure points where my toes rub together or against the front of my trainers. Underneath these, fluid can build up and need aspirating with a needle. Needless to say, like nearly all serious runners I've lost toenails several times. It's something we all accept with pride.

Now I was washed, I was ready for food. It was 4am and still dark, but everyone was full of energy and the wonderful smell of sausages and bacon started to waft towards us. Our hosts, in true Australian fashion, had fired up the barbecue and were cooking us breakfast. It was all delicious washed down with lots of tea. By this point others were finishing, and a jolly gang of us were sitting around the main table. Some people chose to eat before showering, and some even enjoyed a beer from the club bar. It all made for a good atmosphere.

I started to write my diary about how the race had gone. By now, the race times had been uploaded to Facebook, so I tried to work out if I was in the lead overall. My maths was always slightly out, even though it was a simple calculation based on winning margins in three races. I worked out that I had an overall lead of one minute and three seconds, noting in my diary that 'this was not much of a lead!'

At some point we noticed it had got light; morning had arrived. This made it seem even more brutal that some people were still running. There was a round of applause every time someone came in after completing the race, and an especially loud one when seventy-six-year-old Dan brought the race to a close, completing in 6:34.

We were due to leave at 9am, but those post-race hours melted away. Before I knew it, we were packing up our stuff and heading for the bus. I went for a short walk by the river while I ate a snack, just so I could say I had seen Perth in daylight. I must have been tired, but my overwhelming feeling was one of calmness. I was satisfied that I had ticked off another race.

At the airport, I munched on a large blueberry muffin with tea while I caught up on emails. I updated my JustGiving page with some photos of the first couple of races and tweeted thanks for all the donations. The support I was starting to receive on social media was wonderful, and I appreciated it more and more throughout the week.

Soon it was time to get back on our plane and head to Dubai. It was like arriving home when I sat back in seat 41A. I kicked off my shoes, got my book out and pulled the duvet over me. Travelling to Dubai would involve a fuel stop in Columbo, and I hoped to get a good amount of sleep before then.

RACE SUMMARY: PERTH

Positives

- I won again. A win is a win and I'm making the others hurt.
- Heart rate down to 159 [beats per minute] when not in the heat.
- Hamstrings got better through race.
- Listening to music is working well.
- Speed is consistent throughout - virtually no 'no man's land' syndrome today. [This is what I call the section between 15 and 19 miles, when you're well over halfway but a long way from the finish.]
- I am in the lead by a couple of minutes.

Negatives

- Hamstrings so tight - even with stretching on the flight and really good warm-up they will not loosen off.
- Blisters - need the blisters on the ball of my left foot and under the nail of my second toe not to get worse - aspirate on the plane. [I added a postscript saying, 'did get better!']
- Am I running too fast? Will find out in Dubai.

TEXTS AFTER PERTH MARATHON

Just done 3:19 in Perth – 1st place. Hamstrings are tight but I warmed up as much as I could, and they got a bit better and I'm stretching now before a shower. It was a lovely flat night-time run – my fav!! Feeling great!! S

> Well done Susannah!! Great running. Recover well. Just worried you are going too fast. But I know how strong you are. Pace yourself in the hot ones. When is the next one? How many hours' rest? Very happy for you! Mike

I know what you mean about the speed but my legs feel better when I press on – and now I am running well I want to keep it up. Two small blisters on feet but they will dry out fine as we have 12 hours of flying to Dubai so a good rest. The Aussies have fired up the BBQ so eating lots of food. If I can do one more decent one I hope Kristina will give up… but let's see!! S

14
Dubai, UEA (Asia): Still Cruising

The midway point

Dubai was an important milestone in the World Marathon Challenge, as it marked the middle of the journey. Everything from the second half of the Dubai Marathon onwards would be taking us home towards the finish line in Miami.

Dubai also held the promise of a bed. The aim was to land in the early evening and start running at around 8.30pm. At least some of the runners would then be able to have a few hours of sleep before we left at 9am the next day. However, when we landed and our phones and watches set themselves to local time, we realised it was much later than our scheduled time of 6.30pm. This meant we would be able to run in the cool of the night, but it also made getting any time in a real bed much less likely.

The two flights to Dubai had gone smoothly. I had slept when I could but was always awake when food came round. This was all good, but the portions were inevitably smaller than most of us would eat at home. I needed to eat around 5,000 calories a day, but despite clearing my plate and snacking regularly I wasn't quite managing it.

I had been to Dubai to run the marathon in January 2015, so I knew roughly what to expect. Once through arrivals, we were split on to two buses according to where we were staying. Everyone on my bus was headed for the Jumeirah Beach complex, which was only a couple of hundred metres from the start of the race. Everyone else was slightly further away. They would be brought to the start by bus once they had checked in.

I was allocated a room in a villa with four other runners, including Kristina. Everyone at the hotel did their best to get things sorted, and soon I had handed over my passport in exchange for a swipe card for the villa. I based myself in a large double room on the top floor. Putting my washbag in the bathroom and cleaning my teeth in a proper basin felt like a real luxury compared with using the tiny bathroom on the plane. I pulled out a fresh set of kit, which was the same style as I'd worn in Perth and Cape Town but included a black running top instead of a pink one. I try to avoid black if running in a warm climate because it absorbs the heat, but here it would be night time, so it didn't really matter.

Once I was ready, I went outside and found the others gathering by the main gates to the complex. We were told that the start was a couple of hundred metres to our right and that we should be ready to go in the next fifteen minutes. Knowing this meant at least half an hour in practice, I started my usual warm-up routine. I was nicely surprised by how good my legs felt. They were undoubtedly heavy, but they felt like a pair and my hamstrings and glutes felt much more relaxed than they had in Perth.

This race was to be run on the green running track that runs all the way along the beach front. It feels a bit like an athletics track but slightly more spongy. When I had read this in the information that Richard had sent, I thought it would be great: it would be softer on the legs than another 26 miles on hard tarmac. However, Mike had said it would be tougher to run on and I needed to be ready to deal with that. As I jogged down to the start, I couldn't really understand what Mike meant, as the surface felt good to me.

This race was to consist of fifteen loops. Each loop headed 1.4 kilometres up the beach, turned around and headed back to the start to make a loop of 2.8 kilometres. A table of drinks and sweets was provided at the start, and water was available at the far end of the course, giving ample opportunities to keep hydrated.

I connected my MP3 player and got ready to race again.

The race

This race started at 12.45am. It followed the same pattern as Perth, with me going out in front and Stéphanie and Kristina not far behind. The night temperature was perfect, and everything was so peaceful. The bright lights of the hotels and villas lit up the beach front, and the waves rolled gently up the beach. The only people about were those making their way home after late dinners. Their only reaction was to give us a few puzzled looks.

I tried to get into a solid rhythm, but I was already struggling on the running track. Its spongy surface was sucking the energy out of me. Rather than rolling nicely from stride to stride, it was hard work. All my energy was disappearing out through the bottom of my feet and into the track.

As we came to the end of the first lap, I noticed Michael was running on the thin concrete strip between the running track and the wooden planks of the beach walk. It was only a foot and a half wide, but it was wide enough to run on. I followed Michael's lead and switched to the concrete strip – and it was a revelation. Its firm base suited me much better; my whole body felt lighter and my strides were easier. I would stick to the strip for the rest of the race.

Most of the others seemed content to stay on the running track, but some joined me and Michael on the concrete strip. We worked on the basis that a slower runner gave way to a faster runner. I made sure to step off the strip when Michael came whizzing by, and the other men moved off it for me as they were going slower. Kristina, Stéphanie and I all chose our own approach. While I was wedded to the concrete, Stéphanie stayed on the running track – and Kristina was the only person to run on the wooden boardwalk on the other side of the concrete strip. Afterwards, she said it was the nearest thing to a trail, which she enjoyed so much.

Now I had found the concrete strip I was content to get on with pushing out the miles. Only one other danger emerged, and that was at the turnarounds at the end of each 1.4-kilometre stretch. For each of these I had to go back on to the running track, which was wet and slippery with spilled drinks. My right knee, with its lack of cartilage, is not keen on sudden changes of direction and lets me know with a shooting pain. On a couple of early turns I went too fast, and my knee felt sore as I set off in the opposite direction. After that I decided to take the turns really slowly and always turn to my left, so I was pivoting on my good knee, and then accelerate away in a straight line. Once I got the hang of this, it worked well.

The halfway point was not only a milestone for this race but for the whole World Marathon Challenge.

As I turned after seven and a half laps, I thought, 'All I have to do now is everything I have just done!' My mood was also lifted by my 600-metre lead over Stéphanie, with Kristina behind her. It felt comfortable and I was swinging along nicely. My thoughts wandered so much that I can't remember what music I listened to that night.

By the final couple of laps, I was ready for the race to be over. My lead had extended and for the first time I thought Stéphanie looked tired. She seemed to be working hard to stay ahead of Kristina, who looked as tidy and compact as ever. Running into the turn for the final 2.8-kilometre lap I took a deep breath to ready myself for a last push up the beach and back. Michael had already finished and was standing by the drinks table; he gave me a high five as I grabbed some water and pushed on. It's amazing how much the small acts of others – like a high five from a fellow runner – can boost your morale and give you the energy you need to see a race out.

I came into the finish so quickly that the organisers nearly missed getting the tape out in time. My time was 3:26:23 and I felt great, like the race hadn't taken much out of me at all. I said a few words on camera about being four races down with three to go, and posed for some more pictures. Almost seven minutes after I had finished, Stéphanie crossed the line, followed three minutes later by Kristina. By then I had realised how sweaty my top was and that I was starting to get cold. I didn't have any extra layers with me at the finish, so I headed back to my room.

Breakfast but no bed

The luxury of a big hotel room hit me again as I walked in. I followed the usual pattern of having a good stretch before washing. I would have loved a cup of tea, but there was nothing in the villa so I made do with water.

I felt remarkably good, considering that I had now run well over 100 miles at race pace in less than 90 hours. Even so, I could feel a slight ache in the knees. I knew an ice bath would do them the world of good. I started to run a bath but, as you would expect in Dubai, it was not very cold. What I needed was ice, and lots of it.

I grabbed my bin and went across to the main hotel foyer. It was just before 4am so there was no one about, but behind the bar was a huge dispenser of ice. Using my hands, I filled the bin with as much ice as I could. I took it back to my room and chucked it in the cold bath. It was cold enough to make me wince when I got in, but not really cold enough to aid recovery. After the bath I switched to the shower, washing my hair and scrubbing myself until I felt clean. Pulling on a clean t-shirt and some tracksuit bottoms, I felt marvellous. With nothing else to do for a bit, I settled down to write my diary.

By 6am I was absolutely starving; my stomach was gurgling loudly. I was also craving Marmite. I had brought that with me, so all I needed was for breakfast to open. I went across to the hotel at 6.25am in the hope that it might open at 6.30am, and to my delight it did indeed. I hooked my laptop up to the Wi-Fi and made myself the first of several cups of tea before starting to eat. I helped myself to hash browns, tomatoes and beans with a couple of slices of Marmite toast. I then went back for seconds, finishing with a big plate of fruit.

As I munched my way through that sizeable breakfast, other runners came to join me. We all enjoyed the luxury of our civilised surroundings. I must have sat there until 8.30am, when it was time to pack up and get back on the bus. Although most of us had not made use of our beds, it was still great to have had some time out at the hotel. We would appreciate this even more after the next marathon in Madrid, where the facilities were far less luxurious.

RACE SUMMARY: DUBAI

Positives

- Another win with lead extended.
- Got into a strong relentless rhythm.
- Food and drink going down well.
- Great cold bath and shower afterwards.

Negatives

- Hamstrings need a lot of foam-rolling.
- Right knee starting to send out signals it is not happy. (This was primarily because of the U-turns required twice on each loop of the track as opposed to the running itself.)
- It now definitely gets mental - how strong am I?

TEXTS AFTER DUBAI MARATHON

Home in Dubai in 3:26:23. Hamstrings better this time but going to have a cold bath now before the real work starts! Still feeling good!!! S

> Well done Susannah, you are running some great times, how are you feeling? Mike

Hi Mike, you were right about the squidgy running track which was horrid but luckily there was a concrete strip alongside it which Michael (the fastest guy) and I went up and down while everyone else went on the track. My hamstrings have given up complaining which is great but knees feel a bit tired. The cold bath helped and need a sleep on the plane and should be good to go. All aches are equal in both legs which feels good and technique seems to be holding up so it's the mental game now! S

> Good running and great strategy! It's always good to be prepared. Now it's more mental than physical, but warm up well and keep to your routines, you are getting stronger, the sleep will help but again use your mantras when running. Very proud of you – there is a lot more to come. Mike

15
Madrid, Spain (Europe): The Duel

TEXTS BEFORE MADRID MARATHON

Just landed in Madrid and starting to sleep like a log on the plane! Fell asleep with ice on my knees and they feel really cold and hard now so are hopefully ready to go. Definitely a massive warm-up and then I don't need to do anything spectacular, just the same thing I've done loads of times… the support is amazing. S

> Good to hear you slept well. Yes, good warm-up and don't try and race too quickly, give yourself time to get the 'Susannah running machine' going. You are doing brilliantly, just remember the routines and the warm-up. Mike

The mental challenge begins

Understandably, everyone seemed tired after the fourth marathon and it was a quiet bus ride to the airport. I caught myself nodding off, but managed to stay awake: I wanted to fall asleep properly during our single eight-hour flight to Madrid.

Richard had told us that under European regulations, we were going to be allowed to leave our bags in the main luggage hold on the plane while we were in Madrid. We needed to make sure we had everything we needed for the next marathon in our hand luggage. I made the bold choice of taking just a running vest and shorts, despite knowing it would be cold. This decision nearly came back to haunt me.

Lunch consisted of Lebanese-style vegetarian Salouna and chocolate cheesecake. By now I had no issues with sleeping in the air and nodded off easily. Typically, I was awake four hours later: I needed to move to stop my legs cramping, and I was hungry and thirsty again. Before landing we were served roasted vegetable paninis, which were hot and filling. I felt ready to go as we landed in Madrid.

From day one of training, Mike had told me he could train me for the first four marathons, but the rest would be in my head. They would be as much a mental challenge as a physical one, and this was something I had to be ready for. I had written this down and repeated it numerous times to myself and anyone who wanted to discuss the World Marathon Challenge. It was hardwired into my thinking and had become something I was more than ready for. I knew the toughest work was about to begin and found myself looking forward to it. This is what I had trained for, and this is when I would make it count.

Having won the female category for the previous three marathons, I had lulled myself into a false sense of security about the situation with Kristina and Stéphanie. I was naive to think that two capable and competitive professional athletes were just going to sit back and let me win the remaining races. That's not a mistake I will ever make again, and I was lucky to have Mike's support by text message to keep me focused.

We changed into our running gear at the airport. Our bus sped through central Madrid and out the other side to the Jarama Formula One circuit. We had another warm welcome from the local organisers, who showed no irritation that we were two hours late. They showed us to a big room with lots of tables and chairs; this would be our base for the event. After putting my stuff on a chair, I went outside to warm up and see how my body was feeling.

By the time I had finished, I felt as ready to run as I would ever be. I headed back to get my headband and MP3 player, joining everyone else in the pit lane where the start/finish area was set up. Alongside it was the usual table of drinks and treats. Some of the runners had visiting supporters, and there was a good buzz in the cold evening air.

The race

At the pre-race briefing, Richard told us the race would consist of just under eleven laps of the track, starting about 100 metres in front of the finish line. Other runners who had looked at the course in more detail than me talked about the two tough hills on each lap. I tried not to listen and told myself that it would be the same for everyone.

The race started at 8.12pm, and I went off in my usual position behind Michael and tried to get moving as smoothly as I could – get the 'Susannah running machine' going like Mike had told me. As it was only just above freezing, I realised I was going to need to run at a good pace just to keep warm. Most of the other runners had sensibly chosen to wear more layers than me. For the first few miles, I worried that I'd made an error in not wearing long sleeves and gloves. Even as I started to sweat, my muscles and joints felt tighter than usual because of the cold. But it was too late to do anything about that, so I put it to the back of my mind and focused on running.

The first circuit revealed lots of twists and turns in the track. The camber of the road threw me towards the inside of the bend – lovely if you're driving a fast car, but hard work on the legs! The first of the two hills was a significant 100-metre pull that left me puffing hard when the track levelled out and then headed slightly downhill into a right-hand bend. The second hill was not as long or steep, but still made us all work hard. Each circuit finished with a downhill right-hand bend into the pit lane, which set me up well for the start of the next lap. My knees were not enjoying the cold or the undulations, but they were going to have to cope over the next three hours.

It became clear in the first mile that this race would follow a different pattern from the previous three marathons. Rather than having some space to settle into a rhythm, I had Kristina hard on my heels and more than holding her own. As we came into the pit lane to complete the first circuit, to my surprise Kristina moved past on my left-hand side. Like me, she was dressed all in black – but sensibly, she had a hat, long sleeves and leggings and looked to be moving well.

I told myself 'There's no need to panic, just sit behind her and see how the race develops.' At this point Kristina seemed to pick up the pace, and it was all I could do to stay with her. There were no mile markers, but based on the time for each lap and my experience of what different speeds feel like, I reckoned we were travelling at just outside three-hour marathon pace. I didn't think it could last. It was simply bizarre, and almost reckless, to be running this fast.

The second, third and fourth circuits all flew by, with me clinging to Kristina's heels. A pattern was emerging on each lap. I could hold my own on the flat sections and felt almost comfortable on the downhills, but I was struggling on the two uphills. Each time we reached the first steep incline, Kristina would push on and I would not be able to keep up. A gap of 10 or 20 metres would open up, which I would then have to close on the next section of the course. I kept thinking that we could not keep this pace up; I was holding on for a time when it would drop a bit. It never did!

At the end of each lap I grabbed some energy drink and a chewy sweet from the refreshment table, but because I had to do it so quickly I was probably not taking in as much fluid as I should. Equally, the cold was likely to be minimising fluid loss so I hoped everything was balancing out. As we approached the end of the fifth lap, almost the halfway point, we had settled into our formation. I was almost enjoying following Kristina, as I could use her pace and energy to set the rhythm. By this stage we had started to lap other runners, who were surprised to see us travelling so quickly. They told us afterwards that it was epic to watch us racing so hard, which was a great compliment to both of us.

Then things suddenly changed. We were out on lap 6 and heading for the first incline when Kristina started to move away from me. As we went up the hill the gap between us grew. I knew I hadn't dropped my pace, so I quickly realised this was her big race push. She was trying to get away from me, and she was rapidly succeeding. The gap must have been 40 or 50 metres by the time we were halfway up the incline, and it was only getting wider.

Perhaps I should have been panicking, but I remember feeling really calm. It was as if everything was happening in slow motion and I had all the time in the world to consider my options. In reality, there were only two: I could let Kristina get away from me and settle for minimising how far she won by, or I could take her on.

I had between five and ten seconds to make my decision, or Kristina would have made it for me by being too far ahead to catch. In this short space of time a million thoughts went through my head. Did it matter if I came second, given I'd already won three races? Would it even be right and fair to let Kristina win this race? But the thought that stuck in my head at this crucial moment was simply: what would AP do?

Anyone who is a horseracing fan will know what I mean by this – but let me explain. To me, Sir AP McCoy is the greatest jockey there has ever been. Displaying unbelievable levels of grit and determination, he was Champion Jump Jockey for nineteen consecutive years. He's the most admired competitor of his, or potentially any, generation. To achieve this, he put his mind and body through the most gruelling regime. To keep his weight down, he didn't eat much and sweated in hot baths and saunas every day. On many occasions he went out to ride in races still bruised, battered and broken from falls that would have put the rest of us in hospital. We talk about GOAT in sport – the Greatest of All Time – and AP is simply the definition of this.

So, I simply thought: what would AP do? Would he let a fellow competitor get away from him while he still had air in his lungs and energy in his legs? Or would he push back with all he had until he was eventually victorious?

I made up my mind to follow the lead of AP, a genuine hero of mine. I took one massive breath and pushed up the hill with every ounce of energy I could muster. As we got near the top, I was starting to close the gap, which gave me the confidence to press on. The track levelled out and I was able to draw back up behind Kristina. I was breathing hard but couldn't hear the extent of my puffing thanks to the 90s dance music that was blasting into my ears.

Kristina must have been aware of my presence, but she didn't look around or give away any sign that she was worried. She's a professional and I wouldn't have expected her to, but every runner looks for the tell-tale signs that suggest another runner is just that bit more tired than they are. I sat on her right shoulder, as I wanted to let her know that her big mid-race push hadn't worked; I was still here. Just as crucially, I needed time to get some extra oxygen into my lungs and keep myself mentally strong before I considered my next move.

I had managed to see off her big push, but I knew it would only be a matter of time until she made another one and I doubted I could keep fighting back. We were moving into the second half of the race and I decided that I had to push on and get some space between me and Kristina. Only by doing this could I get control of the race.

As we ran down towards a right-hand bend, I took another deep breath and pushed again. I pushed harder than I had ever pushed before. I went up through the gear box until I found a sixth gear I didn't know I had. I didn't look back once to see if the push was working. I didn't think, I just ran. I flew down into the pit lane to complete the sixth lap. Although I wanted to maintain my momentum, I knew I needed some energy and fluids. I charged at the table and nearly took out a fellow competitor (I apologised afterwards!).

As I pushed into the first bend on the next lap, I had a chance to see if my push had worked. The bend almost came back on itself and while I have never been a runner to look behind me, I couldn't help but steal a glance to my right. I saw there must have been nearly 100 metres between us. The push had worked. I was out in front!

Now the long hard work began. There was no one to pace me and the only boost I could look for was lapping people, which would give me no indication of where I was in relation to Kristina. As I climbed the first hill, I realised my big push had taken its toll. By working so hard I had ruined the equilibrium you look for in long-distance running, where you're able to get enough oxygen into your system to clear the lactic acid being produced in your muscles. Over the last ten to fifteen minutes I had produced far more lactic acid than I could hope to clear. Even through my pace had now dropped a bit, I was still in an oxygen deficit, which made my muscles ache. However, this was balanced with the mental boost of being in the lead and seemingly in control of the race.

I don't remember much about laps 7, 8 and 9, other than working hard and moving well. By running so strongly I was keeping the cold at bay, but I was conscious that – for the first time while running – my knees felt tight. The lubricating fluid in my joints wasn't working as well as it had in the warm climates. My legs found the undulations of the track unforgiving, and I could not help but wonder what damage this was doing for the final two races. I knew I would feel sore when I finished.

As I came through the pit lane to complete lap 9 and head out for the penultimate circuit, I started to let myself think about the end of the race. My glance back at the first corner confirmed the lead was still over 100 metres. If I could get out on the final circuit in front then there was no way Kristina could come back at me, as I am always strong at the end of a race. While I was still working hard, I allowed myself a few smiles to relax me. I told myself I was strong and I was loving this, as per my learned mantra.

Heading into the final lap, I was ready for the race to be over. I'd done what I needed to do; it was just a case of getting up those two hills for the final time and staying in one piece to cross the line. At the first bend my lead had dropped but was still around 80 metres – comfortable enough, given that I had less than 4 kilometres to run.

I gritted my teeth and pushed up the first hill, thinking 'this is the last time I ever have to do this'; my thoughts were exactly the same for the second hill. I needed to keep pushing but cruise for home, as I was still in control. Perhaps I'd got so comfortable with the idea of another victory that I'd lost focus.

As I swung down the final hill with the pit lane and finish line in sight, I felt a presence on my right-hand side. I couldn't think what it was. As I looked to the right I did the most massive double take: it was Kristina! In that single moment of horror, I couldn't understand how she had caught me up so rapidly. Before I could think about it too much my flight instincts kicked in and my brain my told me: 'Run!'

169

As if I was running for my life, I surged forward into a sprint. So did Kristina. She hadn't looked at me at all; she was simply running as hard as she could, focused on the line. She'd caught me napping and was hoping to outsprint me in the final 200 metres. Given my lack of sprinting prowess, I'd probably have backed her in this situation. She was on a roll with the high of having caught me, and I was on the back foot having been caught.

However, I found something extra when I needed it, and my legs picked up the speed. The muscle memory and cardiovascular fitness I had developed through the months of sprint intervals between October and January had made a difference. As we sprinted onwards, it was clear I was holding my own. Kristina was not able to get past me, but equally I was not getting away from her. My lungs might have been burning, but I was getting taller and stronger. Every stride we sprinted made me more determined that this would be mine. With 100 metres to go, and after 150 metres at maximum effort, I felt Kristina drop back and admit defeat. She'd come to take victory but yet again, I had managed to fight back and hold on. I pushed on for the line. When I crossed it I had never been so glad to be able to stop running.

On this occasion there was no thumbs up to the camera or brief interview to the film crew. I found myself bent over with my hands on my knees. All I could do was keep breathing in as much air as possible. I turned back in time to see Kristina crossing the line in what would be a new personal best for her: 3:12:02. I hadn't even looked at the clock as I crossed the line, but it had read 3:11:49. Only thirteen seconds between us and just over thirteen minutes outside my best time at that point.

Any duel or competitive battle in sport is about both participants, not just the victor. I felt strongly that my time would not have been anywhere near as fast without Kristina's presence. Without the fierce rivalry I would have struggled to get much below 3:30 on a tough track on a cold night. The joy of competition makes us do things we don't know we're capable of until we've done them.

I went over to Kristina and said something along the lines of 'Bloody hell, where did that come from?' We hugged to show there were no hard feelings, and the duel was done. By then I was able to give a brief interview in front of the camera. I tried in one minute to explain what I later took several pages to write up.

I had promised to keep the family up to date as much as I could. It was about 10pm in the UK, so I got my phone out and called my dad. As he sat by the fire at home, I tried to explain what had happened in a succinct fashion. I'm not sure he got the details beyond another win – which was the most important bit, I suppose.

My phone buzzed with WhatsApp, text and Twitter messages, so I replied to those from my two brothers, friends and work colleagues. I didn't know about it at the time, but they were closely following the Facebook posts that World Marathon Challenge were publishing during and after races. I reported back that it had been an epic race and I had won by thirteen seconds. What I didn't say was that my right knee was painful and my whole body felt incredibly tired after what I had just put it through. Somehow, I needed to get myself ready for yet another marathon.

Cold showers and tuna sandwiches

I stuck with what I knew would work. First, I had a good stretch. Back in the warmth of our big room, everything felt a little bit better – except my right knee, which felt tight and sore. As I prepared to find the showers, Kristina came back to report that there was no hot water. The showers weren't just cold, they were icy cold. She'd decided against using them, but I couldn't bear the idea of being sweaty all the way to Santiago so I went to investigate.

The shower unit was basic but functional. Water appeared to be everywhere; I had to be careful not to slip, which is a challenge when you're tired, aching and carrying a bag. I carefully placed my bag on a chair to keep everything dry, got some shampoo out of my washbag and headed for a cubicle. The water was absolutely freezing – exactly what my sore knee needed to assist its recovery, and it would do the rest of me no harm at all.

I used the 'counting down from five rule' and got under the freezing water just after I had said 'one'. I tried to keep my head out of it to avoid a 'brain freeze', but the rest my body didn't mind it at all. In fact, I could feel it helping my muscles recover. I made myself stay under the water for as long as I could bear. As I stepped out of the cubicle with my teeth chattering, I felt a bit less sore. Before I could start to dress, a female member of the race organiser team passed by to say they had found the switch for the hot water! I went back to the shower, and sure enough, warm water cascaded down. I had another thirty seconds in the shower to warm up a bit and then dressed in my warmest clothes.

I felt clean and ravenously hungry. The organisers had arranged packed dinners for us, but these were rather basic. The main item was a white bread sandwich containing a small amount of tuna mayonnaise and some salad. Luckily, I like tuna, so even though it wasn't exactly what I would have chosen, I started eating. The sandwiches didn't seem popular so I ended up getting through three of them, which helped replace some of the energy I'd lost. If I was to do the World Marathon Challenge again, I would pack a nice pot of noodles to hydrate with hot water from the ancient kettle that was available to us all. As it was, I survived just fine on my midnight snack of white bread and hot herbal tea.

We had the entire night to wait for everyone to finish and get back to the airport. I settled into my post-race routine of writing my diary and chatting to other runners as they completed. Many others started to doze in chairs or on the floor, but once again I didn't feel that tired. I was still elated that I had run such a strong race. I also wanted to keep moving so I could see how my body felt. I was pleased to find that the aching was evenly distributed, and my sore right knee seemed to be settling down.

Everyone who finished had found Madrid a hard race. The undulations of the track had made this much more difficult than the previous three marathons, which had all been flat. But it was also the first time we dared to think about getting to Miami and the finishing line – in less than forty-eight hours' time. On the bus back to the airport, tiredness and optimism seemed to be present across the group in equal measure.

RACE SUMMARY: MADRID

Positives

- I won! In a really hard race - with a sprint finish.
- I learned to sit behind Kristina, then make a move = tactics.
- Food/drink all good.

Negatives

- I ran much harder than I wanted to in order to win.
- Knees really didn't like hills and cold - how will they recover?
- What is left in the tank?

TEXTS AFTER MADRID MARATHON

Oh crikey Mike it was a tough race! The F1 circuit had 2 hills and lots of long slopes which were hard on the legs – along with it being pretty cold. Warm-up worked well though so felt good going off but Kristina went off so hard, but I sat behind her and tried not to race. Then made a big move before half way and got the lead for the rest of the race only for her to surprise me on the last lap and come up alongside me with 150m to go so I did a sprint finish to win by 13 seconds!! Time was 3:11:49 so too quick. Showers were cold but this was great for my legs and have compression tights on so feel ok. My cumulative lead with 2 races to go is 13:04 which I just hope is enough. Today was epic – I could have settled for 2nd but something in me wouldn't let me do it!! Time to recover. S

Hey Susannah, it's called GRIT, and you have it in buckets! So the strategy will be to stick with her, let her do the running, just sit on her shoulder let her pace you and overtake her if she is slowing down. She is probably planning to go out fast again to break you so warm up well on both. This is about being clever as well as determined. She also left a lot on the course yesterday. Cold showers are good. What time are you flying?

16

Santiago, Chile (South America): Holding It Together

TEXTS BEFORE SANTIAGO MARATHON

First sleep on the plane was disturbed by having to get more food in me but got 2 more 5-hour flights to rest. The legs seem to be recovering but I just hope Kristina doesn't have that in her again as it was hard! The next courses are back to being flat I think so should suit me well. And it will be warm in Santiago and Miami which also helps the joints etc. S

Crossing messages Mike! Yes hoping yesterday has got to have hurt her but I was so naive to think I was safe with a 100m lead and let her come back at me – but I guess that's the difference between a pro and a decent amateur. I won't do that again but with 13 mins banked I can definitely let her do the work – but she's a stage race specialist so don't think she is tiring. S

You have won 4 and come 2nd once so she is more worried. Run your own race just be aware of where she is.You have run brilliantly, and I was very proud of you. Remember your routines and warm up well. Mike

Yup. I can't bear to have worked this hard and then let it go now… hope my stubborn gene just won't let that happen. The warm-up is amazing – the skipping fired everything up and in 12–15 mins it completely changes how my legs feel! No one else seems to warm up much at all bar a couple of stretches – madness!! S

You will win. Mike

Flights... and more flights

Our journey from Madrid was to consist of three flights, with refuelling stops at Tenerife and at Fortaleza in northern Brazil, before landing in Santiago for our penultimate race. This was not the closest place we could have run in South America but it promised the best running experience and plenty of recovery time on the plane.

I was looking forward to some sleep. The lack of Wi-Fi on the plane was a blessing; if I had been constantly connected to the outside world, I would only have been distracted and missed out on sleeping time. As it was, I would get comfortable in my seat, turn my phone off and read my book until I fell asleep – which was taking less and less time as the week progressed.

It was only a couple of hours to Tenerife, so I had a short sleep before we landed. After take-off on the flight to Fortaleza, I enjoyed a full English breakfast. I was really hungry and needed salt, so I didn't feel like waffles with syrup, the vegetarian option. A cooked breakfast never tastes great on a plane, but it filled me up and I was asleep again in no time.

As we landed at Fortaleza, I was starting to get fidgety so I went to have a good look outside from the steps of the plane. Feeling fidgety on a flight is usually annoying, but this time I took it as a positive sign that I had enough energy to fidget. My mind and body were gearing themselves up for the sixth marathon. I was no longer having to consciously prepare myself for the race; it all seemed to be happening automatically. I iced my knees a couple of times and was pleased to find they were cold and hard, as they should be.

On our third flight, I found myself ragingly hungry again. Rather than a proper lunch, we were offered tomato, ham or chorizo bruschetta. A well-made bruschetta is a decent thing, but these were a bit tasteless and, crucially, not calorific enough. I ended up having eight of the tomato ones, followed by a couple of mini cupcakes and a chocolate bar, but I didn't feel full. As I got off the plane, I knew I was not properly fuelled for the race ahead.

A warm Chilean welcome

Santiago airport was crazy. It was a warm evening and people were everywhere. After we'd collected our luggage I changed in the bathrooms at the airport, donning another pair of running shorts and a vest. We had to wait a while to find out where the buses were, so several people went off to find something to eat. I didn't have any local currency and couldn't see anything I particularly wanted, so I made do with 80 grams of Cadbury's chocolate once we got on the bus. I'm a huge fan of chocolate, but it would have been much better to have had some slow-burning carbohydrate-based food. I knew the chocolate would give me a spike in energy, but I worried about what would happen when those energy levels dipped.

The evening traffic in Santiago was busy but it seemed to flow well, and it wasn't long before we were parking up at Parque Arauco, a big park in one of the smart districts of Santiago. Surrounded by impressive buildings, it looked well kept, with wide sandy paths weaving between grass, trees and flowerbeds. I instinctively liked the place.

Just as likeable was the warm welcome from the local race organisers. They seemed genuinely enthused to see us and put up with endless questions, which started with where the nearest loos were. As ever, we were several hours behind schedule so we would not start running until well into the evening. We all took what bags we needed; for me that was all of them, as I wasn't sure where things were packed and felt safer having everything with me. We dumped these in the gazebos at the start/finish area and started to get ready while the organisers erected the start clock and other essentials.

While nothing was seriously hurting, I was aware of feeling very tired. Even after my tried and tested warm-up regime, my legs still felt sore and heavy. For the first time, my left leg was more tired than my right leg – and this would only get worse. I couldn't eat any more, yet I know I hadn't eaten enough for another marathon effort. I was taking a big step into the unknown.

The race

Everyone seemed to look how I felt, but we were all in it together. Richard told us we'd be running fourteen loops of the park. The surface was a sandy hard-base track, perhaps marginally more forgiving than tarmac, but there would be plenty of small inclines, twists and turns – not what you want to be facing on tired legs.

Kristina, Stéphanie and I set off alongside each other. The picture the official photographer took to capture the moment shows I had determination etched all over my face. The course started uphill, then after a couple of turns it sent us up a short sharp incline for about 30 metres before levelling out. All I could think about was that I was going to have to do that another thirteen times! The top section of the course was flat, with the main landmark being a beautiful bridge that we crossed twice. The bridge was wooden with flowers growing all over it and lights in the canopy above. It would have been great to stand and admire it, but there was no time for that. Returning across the bridge we then took a sharp right-hand corner downhill into the final third of the course. My right knee came to hate this turn, and I had to be careful not to land heavily or twist on it any more than I had to. Every one of the fourteen times I took this turn I winced.

The final section of the course saw us running downhill towards the drinks and sweets table, where we shouted out our number to check our loop had been registered. Then we turned back uphill across the finish line to begin another circuit. It was a tricky course to follow: even halfway through the race, I still had to be careful not to take the wrong route.

I focused on getting into a rhythm that would see me through the race in one piece. I was the lead female runner, initially with Stéphanie closest to me but later with Kristina once again chasing me. In the first half of the race I saw Stéphanie and Kristina several times, which meant they were not far behind me. Every time this happened it spurred me on to get moving up the hill to put more distance between us. Running faster was hard work, but it actually helped me feel better. It seemed to lift me off my heavy left side to make running feel a little easier. The challenge was then to maintain speed through the twists and turns.

I got a stitch several times during the race. I knew this was because my body was low on fuel and the engine was starting to sputter. Every time a stitch arrived I took ten deep breaths. The extra air helped clear the oxygen deficit and, just as crucially, took my mind off the stabbing pain in my side. Often, the next time I thought about the stitch it had lessened and I felt under control.

For the first time, I had moments of doubt because I felt so tired. Luckily, like the stitch, these thoughts never lingered long enough to be a serious concern. I focused on one circuit at a time and made sure to get as much energy drink and sweets into myself as possible when I passed the checkpoint. Listening to music did its usual job of overriding the noise of my breathing.

By the final quarter of the race I had built up a comfortable lead. I knew that if I could keep rolling around each circuit, I would take victory number five. In a way, it helped that we all looked tired. No one was springing along; we were all just moving. Kristina and Stéphanie both have much better natural running techniques than mine, but neither of them could go any faster that evening. This was hardly a surprise given how hard we had all worked in Madrid.

I knew this race would be much slower than the previous night, and I crossed the line in 3:37:44. This was nearly five minutes ahead of Kristina and over twelve minutes ahead of Stéphanie. On tired legs, with a body that was rapidly running out of fuel, this was a good effort. Unlike in Madrid, I was able to speak straight to the camera on pulling up. I said that this race had hurt but I didn't care, as we only had one race to go and we'd see everyone in Miami. The next stop really was Miami!

Showers, pizzas and boxing clever

Before we got to Miami, we needed to get everyone across the line in Santiago. By now it was the middle of the night and we were just about the only people still awake. It was still warm enough not to worry about getting cold: a novelty for those of us used to a British climate.

The generous race organisers had ordered boxes and boxes of pizza, but before I ate anything I wanted a shower. I was sweaty and had dust from the sandy path all the way up my legs and in my trainers. The organisers had also arranged for a large pile of lovely fresh white towels to be available, and showed those of us finishing to a local boxing gym with spacious showers. This was only quarter of a mile away but seemed so much further on tired legs.

It's almost worth getting really sweaty and grubby just to enjoy the process of getting clean. After about twenty minutes enjoying the hot water, Stéphanie, Kristina and I emerged feeling like new people. At the same time, some of the men had been showering and as we emerged the temptation to get into the boxing ring was too great for Kristina and Kevin. At this point we all learned that as well as being an excellent runner, Kristina is a decent boxer, easily putting Kevin on the ropes. I caught ten seconds of it on my phone, which Kevin enjoyed posting on social media. Definitely 1:0 to the girls on the boxing front.

Back at the finish area we handed back our damp towels and got busy attacking the pizza. I lost count of the number of pieces I ate, but rarely has cold pizza tasted better. The salty black olives on top were just what I needed, washed down with some Coke Zero – I couldn't face any more water or energy drink.

I sat on a bench with a small trestle table in front of me and started to write in my diary. In the process of doing this, something happened to me for the first time: I got nervous. I started to think about how close I was to winning the World Marathon Challenge. Even more amazingly, I was now in a position to set a new world record. I had over seventeen minutes on Kristina; although that sounds a lot, in a marathon it could disappear quickly if something went wrong. The final race and the world record were mine to lose, but lose them I could easily do.

To keep my mind occupied I kept writing my diary, but I eventually gave in to my growing nervousness and texted Mike. As always, he had the words to explain what I was feeling and how to get through it. Mike explained that how I was feeling was perfectly normal, and that I needed to channel my nervous energy into my lungs and legs. It's difficult to make this simple connection when your brain stops thinking clearly.

I was also getting loads of messages from people at home, which didn't necessary help the nerves but did make me feel loved. I had posted a message on Twitter after each race, as I knew people were following my progress and had made generous donations to my JustGiving page. I couldn't keep up with all the messages, but a few stood out. This one from Rod Street, Chief Executive of Great British Racing and a fellow marathon runner, made me start to realise what I was in the process of achieving.

Rod Street @Rods_Tweet . Feb 6

While we were sleeping @TheIronLadyRuns won her fifth consecutive @WorldMarathon77 in five days. This time in Chile. Form: 211111. One race to go!

She deserves an airport welcome!

#WednesdayMotivation

As I was finishing my writing, Kristina joined me at the opposite end of the table and we got chatting. Even though we got on well, we were competitors and I appreciated this situation must have been tough for her. She had come to win the World Marathon Challenge, and any sensible person would have backed her. Then this unknown amateur runner turns up to ruin the party. If she did feel like this, she never showed it to me, but it's how I would have felt if I had been in her position.

By this point, Santiago was waking up. Everyone had finished the marathon; some were asleep on the bus and a few of us were still outside. I told a couple of the guys how good the showers had been, and they replied with less than complete enthusiasm. It turned out that as the three fastest women, we'd got there first and drained the hot water. Kristina and I agreed that the guys needed to run faster.

Soon it was time for the rest of us to get on the bus. This time I did fall asleep; I simply couldn't keep my eyes open. Santiago Airport was just as crazy in the morning as it had been the previous evening. It seemed to take forever to check in our bags, but eventually I was free to head to the departure gate.

While checking my emails, I was suddenly overcome with the need to eat. I retraced my steps and found a small café where a few others were sitting, including race organiser Richard. I knew we wouldn't be going anywhere without him. My eyes fell on some cheesy pasta in a plastic bowl, which the woman behind the counter microwaved for me. I added orange juice, a big piece of chocolate cake and another Coke Zero to my tray and paid for it on my card in dollars. I didn't even look at the cost; there and then I would have paid anything for hot food. The cheesy pasta tasted like the best thing I had ever eaten and the orange juice was wonderfully refreshing. I had to save the chocolate cake to eat on the plane.

Full of hot food, my mood completely changed. I went from feeling tired and grumpy to happy, positive and ready for the final race in Miami. I also knew I wouldn't need to stay awake for food on the plane, meaning I could sleep for longer. Once on the plane I still felt a little nervous and anxious about the final race, but my priority for now was sleep, which arrived the moment I closed my eyes.

RACE SUMMARY: SANTIAGO

Positives

- I won – and without having to race too hard.
- Got a lead of 18.02 for Miami. [Later I amended this to 17.51 as my calculations had been slightly out all week.]
- Don't think I have added any more aches and pains so game on!

Negatives

- My left leg is hurting more than my right – got to look after this.
- Felt a bit sick at the end, and a stitch during it. The body is tired.
- My lead does NOT make me safe.

TEXTS AFTER SANTIAGO MARATHON

Well done Susannah! As I said you will win! How are you feeling? Cold shower and food and hydration. Text me when you can. Mike

> All good!! It was hard – 14 loops of a twisty circuit in a park with lots of ups and downs but I was in control from the start and won in 3:37 so I think have a 19 min lead for tomorrow. They have got us pizza which I am in desperate need of! Legs aching in all sorts of places but no overriding problems. Put the shower on to cold for my legs and feet so I am learning! S

Great running recover well, Miami's the hardest one! Recover well, focus and be tactical during the race, don't try and win it from the beginning. Kristina has nothing to lose. So keep her in your sight until you are ready to fly! Mike

> I'm 5 pieces of pizza down and starting to come back to life. Kristina admitted she found it hard today after yesterday so I don't think she can pull anything out the bag tomorrow if I can just hold it together. I was nervous before tonight's race which was a new sensation – getting close is nerve wracking. S

Have loads of food. So there are two good lessons. One – you need to run tactically and don't give up until you have won! Two – being nervous is what competition is all about. You need to channel it into the legs, the lungs and the brain. You are a competitor now, you are going to be a winner! Recover well, last one to go, focus and do your routine. I am very proud of you. Mike

> Got it on 1 and 2! The course is dead flat and there will be loads of support in Miami which I know will fire me up. This is the only moment I don't feel we could have planned for – going into the last race with nearly 19 mins in hand and a chance to set a new World Record... I never thought I could do this but I'll make sure I start to believe it right now!! S

Yep, if you believe you can, you can! Just follow your routines. The warm-up will calm you down. Pace the race. Mike

17
Miami, Florida (North America): The Finale

Miami-bound

Our final flight into Miami was just over eight hours long – the perfect amount of time for plenty of sleeping and some more eating.

As usual, I didn't sleep for more than four hours before I needed to get up and move about, but that was going to be enough to get me through the final race. In my diary I had jotted down how good the sleep had been and written several pages about what this was all starting to mean to me. I suspect this was a way of trying to keep the nerves at bay. Despite everything we had planned together, Mike and I had never discussed winning or the world record. And yet I was 26.2 miles away from potentially achieving both.

I iced my knees for a final time, more for something to do than because they needed it. My knees felt cold and exactly how they should. However, my left leg ached a lot. I must have been leaning on it much more than I had realised in the Santiago race. I had to accept that the last race was going to hurt; all I needed to do was get through it in a time I that had run many times before.

I thought that 3:30 would be enough to win it, as I couldn't envisage Kristina being about to run more than nineteen minutes quicker than that to beat me. Her 3:12 marathon in Madrid had been a new personal best for her, so to better that would be a huge effort. Yet I knew she was a fierce competitor, so I needed to be ready for any eventuality. I needed to have confidence in my mental strength, while hoping my body could keep it together.

Our final meal on board was a sweetcorn and tomato salad, followed by a butternut squash tagine with potatoes and vegetables, and completed with an apple tart. Frankly, I just spooned it in; at this stage I just needed calories. As I was digesting my food, the nerves suddenly hit. I felt as if I was made of lead. My brain and body felt frozen in my seat. Recalling my texts with Mike after the previous race, I knew what was happening so I didn't worry. I just stayed in my seat with my duvet over me, trying not to think about much at all. Other people seemed to be wide awake by now, and some were starting to get their kit ready, but I couldn't move. For the first time since Santiago, I wondered if I really did have another marathon in me. I seriously questioned whether I could make my body go through another competitive 26.2 miles at the pace I needed for victory.

After a little while I decided to listen to some music to get me out of my state of nervous lethargy. My World Marathon Challenge song, as cheesy as that sounds, was David Guetta's 'Memories'. It has a great beat and the lyrics seemed relevant to the madness of the journey I was on: 'All the crazy shit I did tonight, those will be the best memories.' It's not Shakespeare, but it helped me to get me back in the game. Once I had listened to it a couple of times and taken some paracetamol for my aching muscles, I felt better.

It was early evening when we started to descend into Miami International Airport. The city looked so busy with long tailbacks of traffic on the highways, but I could also see plenty of areas of water and parks between all the lights. By this stage I had the nerves under control and was in a state of calm. I was ready.

We were at least five hours behind the initial schedule, so it would be another night-time run. The 168-hour time limit did not expire until the next morning, so everyone would have enough time to complete the challenge.

Welcome to Miami

Despite having waited for several hours, the locals greeted us enthusiastically before showing us to the buses. The airport was enormous, but the walking helped to wake up my body. I was in good shape except for my aching left leg. The quad was sore, but of most concern was the tight hamstring. As a runner, you rely on your glutes and hamstrings to propel you forward. My hamstring felt like it could cramp at any second. If it did that when I was running, I would be in serious trouble and my nineteen-minute lead could disappear quickly. As I sat on the bus absorbing the sights of Miami and munching on a Rice Krispies Square, I tried not to think too much.

Many of the runners had friends and family coming to support them for this final leg. I was more than content with the amazing messages and tweets I was getting from home, which meant I never felt like I was running alone. As we stepped on to the pavement at South Beach, everyone who was there to support us went crazy. Feeling a little like being celebrities was a great boost for us all.

As we had been advised, many of us had booked a room in the Bentley South Beach Hotel, which over-looked the start/finish area on the beach front across the road. It was comforting to know that this was the place where this amazing challenge would be con-cluded. There would be no more surprises or new places – this was it.

My hotel room felt like a haven of quietness. I quickly unpacked a few things, putting my washbag in the bathroom so it would feel more like home when I returned in the early hours of the morning. Having changed into my running kit and pinned my final number to my SportsAid vest, it was time to head out and get ready to race.

The warmth of the evening and the buzzing atmo-sphere hit me after the cool peace of my room. The organisers, who are responsible for the Miami mar-athon each year, had an air of supreme efficiency. While the final preparations were being made I did my warm-up and visited the public bathroom. Just before 9.30pm we were called to the start line for our final race.

The final race

Once we were all gathered behind the start, we posed for a final picture. I am sure that many of us now treasure this image – it marks a special moment – but at the time, all I was thinking about was the running ahead of me.

Richard said 'Good luck' to me and I smiled in return, unable to say much. The course would consist of five there-and-back loops, with each loop being just over 8 kilometres. The route followed the sea front and was mainly on the tarmac surface, with some small sections on wooden boardwalk. Reassuringly, it would be completely flat. As well as the drinks and sweets on the table at the start/finish area there would be water midway along each loop and energy drinks at the turnaround point.

I set my MP3 player to a playlist of all my favourite songs, which I had made especially for this race. I knew I would need some good tunes to keep me buzzing along. After a countdown we set off into the Miami evening to the sound of cheers from family and friends who were supporting all of us crazy runners. As usual, Kristina, Stéphanie and I moved off together. The photo shows I was wearing my focused frown; if I had any doubts on the inside, they weren't showing on the outside.

This time the race followed a different pattern. The rest of the leading men all decided to go off really fast. Rather than having a bit of space to myself and thinking about where Kristina and Stéphanie were, I found myself surrounded by other runners. I couldn't understand why they were all choosing to go off so quickly, but then I realised they must have been vying for places. I remember thinking that if they had this much energy left in the tank, they could have just run harder in the previous races.

I recalled Mike's words to me after race four in Dubai: 'don't try and race too quickly, give yourself time to get the "Susannah running machine" going'. The words 'Susannah running machine' went over and over in my mind as I ticked off the first couple of miles. I wanted to get into a rhythm so I could roll from stride to stride at a decent pace while not causing any issues to my left leg.

It became clear early on that I was going to need to use my arms a lot because my legs were tired. Whenever I let my arms drop, my speed would immediately reduce, and everything felt heavier and harder work. My arms were my best friends that evening; they worked just as hard as my heart, lungs and legs in keeping the show on the road.

As we twisted along South Beach, I started to relax a bit. The 'Susannah running machine' was working well and I was out in front. I enjoyed the sections of wooden boardwalk, as they were slightly springy and made a nice contrast to the concrete path.

At the turnaround point, I did my usual slow left-handed turn away from my right knee, taking an energy drink from a volunteer, and headed back towards the start/finish area. This was the perfect opportunity to see where Kristina and Stéphanie were. To my surprise, Stéphanie was really close behind me, with Kristina not much further back. This race was far from mine. I lifted my head and tried to look as if I was running easily, so as not to show any sign of weakness.

There were people out strolling after dinner and a few kids on bikes, but the path was wide enough for everyone. When I was about a kilometre away from the start/finish area I moved to my left to avoid someone and got the fright of my life when I bumped into another person. I turned to see it was Stéphanie! She had closed up on me and was trying to overtake.

I tried not to look flustered, but I wondered how this had happened. Had I dropped my pace? I made myself acknowledge that this was not a disaster: I had over an hour in hand over Stéphanie and I didn't need to beat her. If she wanted to go and win the race, I could still be the overall winner. However, the competitor inside me was having none of this! I gave myself a metaphorical kick in the ribs and told myself to get moving – 'Push, push', as per my mantra. I came into the checkpoint in first place by just a few metres. Grabbing some water, an energy drink and a chewy sweet, I went round the cone and back out for the second loop.

I think this must have been Stéphanie's big push, as she never got close to me again and over the next couple of loops she was overtaken by Kristina. On this second circuit I made the most of the cups of water available halfway along the route: it was a warm evening and I was sweating freely. I had already started the race a bit dehydrated, given the travelling and previous races, so I needed to drink as much as I could.

By this stage my pace and rhythm were solid, if unspectacular. I was breaking the race down into as many parts as I could, with mini checkpoints in my head that I could look forward to reaching. A five-loop course works well for this. Before I knew it, I had completed the second loop and was heading for halfway.

The great thing about starting a race with really tired legs is that they can't get much worse. As I went through halfway, I did a mental check and concluded that I was feeling about the same as I had at the start. I was conscious of the need to overuse my arms to maintain the pace, while not over-striding in case my left hamstring seized up, but I was getting the job done.

The fourth loop was the 'no man's land' part of the race. Here, I just tried to keep my mind on the job. The cheesy pop music blasting into my ears helped, along with the fact that Kristina was only a couple of minutes behind me. Although it's hard to have someone chasing you, it's exactly what you need to keep the pace up and achieve a decent time. There's no doubt I would not have run the times I did across the week without Kristina and Stéphanie's presence.

I vividly remember coming into the checkpoint for the final time. I turned, I said to myself out loud, 'Right, one more bloody loop, see you in a bit!' I love running but there comes a stage in every race when you just want the job done. I was certainly at that point.

I pushed away from the well-wishers and set off along South Beach for the last time. I tried to absorb everything, knowing it might be the first and last time I would ever run here. My mind was racing as hard as my legs, trying to process the previous six days and what was about to happen if I stepped across the finish line once more. I simply could not imagine anything beyond the finish line. The world after that seemed completely blank.

At the final turnaround point my lead on Kristina had shortened a little, but it was safe enough and I pushed for home. With a couple of kilometres to run, I took my earphones out and tucked my MP3 player into the back pocket of my shorts. I wanted to enjoy this moment and absorb all the sights and sounds. The last kilometre seemed to take forever, but eventually the finish line came into sight. I picked up the pace as much as my tired legs could manage.

I crossed the line with my hands in the air in a time of 3:26:24.

Then it hit me. I just needed to cry. I stopped running, bent over, held my face in my hands and gave some big sobs. The feeling was not one of happiness as you might expect, but sheer relief. I had not messed up. I had done it. I was the World Marathon Challenge winner and the new female World Record Holder.

A big slice of pizza and another sleepless night

The next few minutes were a wonderful blur. I got my breath back and drank some water while Richard gave me one medal for completing Miami, another medal for completing all seven races and, best of all, a massive glass trophy to mark my victory. Michael, who is a pro at photoshoots, got me lined up with him on the finish line and there were lots of flashing blubs and clicking cameras.

At this point I realised Kristina had crossed the line. When I looked back at the times, I realised she had finished only one minute and eleven seconds behind me. She had been coming back at me on the final loop without me really knowing. She was a true competitor right to the end, and I have massive respect for that. Stéphanie was only seven minutes behind Kristina, which rounded off impressive performances for the top three women: we finished third, fourth and seventh in the overall standings.

Dave Painter, who had been filming all week and had been kind and supportive throughout, asked if we could record a piece to camera. We found a quiet spot and I talked through what had happened over the previous week. I finished by saying 'and I still love running!' That was the absolute truth. None of the miles had reduced my love of this purest of sports.

On returning to the finish, I spied an enormous pizza box and asked if I might be able to have a slice. One of the organising team told me to help myself, so I immediately got stuck into an absolutely delicious slice of pepperoni pizza. I sat on the wall by the finish so I could take the weight off my legs and watch the other runners finishing. I turned on my phone and thought about tweeting something, but I couldn't think what to say. But Dave was super-quick in editing my short interview, so I re-tweeted that with the following comment:

Susannah Gill @TheIronLadyRuns · Feb 7
I did it!!!!

Miami marathon done @WorldMarathon77!!

Finished 777 with a 3:26:24 marathon along South Beach and set a new World Record in the process!!

What a week!! Thank you for all the support along the way and donations to @TeamSportsAid. #marathon777

> **HUTC** @HUTCTV
> Congratulations to Britain's Susannah Gill @TheIronLadyRuns who has just won the women's title for the @WorldMarathon77 - in Miami this morning, setting a new World record for the event. @mikebreakfast

The moment I did this it received a big reaction. By now it was about 7am in the UK and everyone was getting up. I hadn't known how many people in the running world, along with friends, family and colleagues, had been tracking the progress of the World Marathon Challenge. Now they got to see the final result and it produced a lot of 'likes'!

Just as I was thinking about heading to the hotel, I got a message from Frank Keogh at BBC Sport. I knew him through work, and he'd seen the news and wondered if we could speak. I said I'd be delighted to, as I had nothing else to do now there was no race to prepare for. We must have chatted for about fifteen minutes. In the wonderful haze of endorphins, I just said exactly what I felt and hoped it would make sense to others. Frank and his BBC colleague Laura Savvas published the piece on the front page of the sports page under the headline 'World Marathon Challenge: Britain's Susannah Gill wins after runs in seven continents'. The article would go on to be shared by many other media outlets.

The first person I had to text was Mike. We'd worked on this together, and not for one moment did I feel I was doing it alone. If I had failed in this final race, I would have been gutted for myself but devasted to have let down Mike and The Running School team. They had all been such an important part of my achievement.

TEXTS AFTER MIAMI MARATHON
I've done it!!!! 3:26:24 – you've coached the new 777 female World Record holder. I'm celebrating with the biggest slice of pizza I've ever had! S

> Well done very proud of you!! I am looking at the reports now. Brilliant achievement. How's the pizza and how are you feeling? Mike

Feeling good – ready for No. 8... jokes. Been chatting to BBC and Twitter is going nuts! Time for a shower and I guess sleep. Can I come next week and start the repair process? My left leg was very heavy in [marathons] 6 and 7 as I seemed to be leaning on it but actually got better in the second half of the race today as kept trying to lift up my left heel and get my weight onto the right leg. Had such a great rhythm with my arms today – kept me going all the way! S

> Yep you need a lot of sleep. Absolutely next week, when are you landing back? Recovery starts next week and I will send you an email with some ideas. On the plane I want you to think about what next. Ultras or break the age group pb for half and marathon and 50k!!

I look forward to catching up. Oh and how about a book with your coach '24 weeks to the world marathon challenge win'? Mike

OMG I had exactly the same thoughts about a book as it would be super fun to write and everyone wants training programmes and advice. Definitely want to do a faster marathon, then I'm not sure. Flying back at 5pm Miami time today so got some time to chill – and try and sort the mountain of dirty kit out ready for washing. Would Monday evening suit? I could do 6pm or 7pm (got a meeting until 5pm)? S

Yes Monday is good at 6pm and we can start recovery. Eat well and safe trip back. Mike

Perfecto – will stop me doing something stupid like getting straight back on the treadmill! Doing some interviews with BBC etc so Running School will be getting a few mentions. No idea how far I would have got if I had tried to take this on without your advice and expertise, but I know this would not have been the outcome!! S

It was a team effort but you did all the work!! You are by far the strongest athlete mentally I have worked with and that includes all the Olympic and gold medallists!!

Gosh – they all need to get tougher then! S

The texts from my brothers, friends and colleagues started rolling in. I responded to each and every one of them: I was so touched that so many people cared about what I'd just done. By this stage I was getting cold. With most of the others having crossed the line, it was time to go back to the hotel room. Happily, before the sun started to come up, every competitor had successfully completed the World Marathon Challenge.

It was about 3am but I thought I'd sit up for a while and reply to some more messages, then have a shower and maybe a rest. I eventually had a shower at 11.30am! It might sound ridiculous, but there was so much to do. The messages flooded in and I gave a BBC interview over Skype, where I must have looked rather sweaty. I wrote a blog for Racing Together, a British horseracing charity who'd featured me before I went away, and updated my JustGiving page with new photos and information. I suppose I didn't need to do all these things, but having come this far I wanted to complete the job properly. I also wanted people to know how much their support meant to me.

I craved a cup of tea, but with no milk in my room I made do with water. The bed looked lovely but the nearest I got to it was using it as a base for repacking my bags. After adding my medals and the sizeable trophy I was relieved that my bags would safely zip up. I asked the hotel to book me a taxi for 2pm to take me to the airport for my 5pm flight. Then I wandered down to South Beach for lunch. I found a cheerful restaurant on the beach front and asked for a large margarita. Of course, this was the size of four cocktails in the UK. I took a couple of mouthfuls and started to relax. The messages kept coming, and I spoke to another journalist over lunch.

Once at the airport I had a spare hour to write my diary. Doing this made it all start to feel a bit more real with memories, faces, places and races all whizzing through my mind. On the flight back to London I re-read everything I had written throughout the week. It was like reading the diary of someone else. It was all familiar, but the tough competitor who had written every word didn't seem quite like me. I knew I was competitive, but I had not known quite how far I was willing to push myself. The World Marathon Challenge taught me I will push myself as far as is needed, and just a little further.

RACE SUMMARY: MIAMI

Positives

- I won!! That was the aim!
- I used my arms really well to set the rhythm – most of the time!!
- Got so good at eating and drinking during the race – no hypos for me [Here I was referring to low sugar levels, which diabetics can suffer from – I was stealing language from my diabetic brother, which had become familiar to me over the last twelve years].

Negatives

- Left leg was so tired and sore – makes me think it could never do JOGLE [John O'Groats to Land's End] or another crazy ultra.

- Seemed very thirsty – do I drink enough?

Conclusion

Getting back to 'normal'

The most startling thing that has happened since the World Marathon Challenge is that people want to talk to me about running. No one had ever really wanted to do that before aside from friends and family, who probably felt they had to.

The hours and days after returning home were filled with talking about running. On the Friday morning I got back, I found myself on the BBC News with Annita McVeigh at 12.30pm, followed by the World News at 2.30pm and finally Euronews at 6.30pm. By now I was more than ready for my first night in a bed for nine days.

There was far more press coverage than I had ever expected. In one surreal moment I saw that my name was the first answer in the *Guardian*'s weekly sports quiz, sitting alongside questions about sportspeople who were 'actually' famous. In interviews, the only tough question was 'And what next?' The World Marathon Challenge had been the biggest and best adventure I could have hoped for. It was tough to imagine what could top it – and perhaps nothing will.

The endorphin high created by running so far in one week, with such an incredible finale, was immense. Even by the time I returned to work I felt like I was floating. I didn't even seem to feel tired. I was simply very happy.

Alas, as every runner knows, endorphins cannot last forever. About three weeks after returning, I switched from being happy about what I had achieved to feeling negative. My brain was stuck in a cycle of thinking about all the things that could have gone wrong. What if I had been able to win race 5 in Madrid? What if my hamstring had cramped in Miami? What if Kristina had caught me in that last race and I'd lost the whole thing by as little as a minute? All these possibilities were plausible. I hadn't worried about them at the time, yet now they would not leave me alone.

As I had done so many times before, I turned to Mike. He didn't seem surprised. He had already told me that I needed to look after myself and that I would get tired and probably ill at some point. Sure enough, I had got a cold, but I hadn't felt tired. When that suddenly changed, Mike was there to support me.

As ever, Mike had the answer – just not the one I wanted. I said I wanted a 'reset' button so I could feel as fresh as I had before the World Marathon Challenge. He explained that what I was feeling was an inevitable consequence of achieving such a tough goal. Crucially, he reassured me that most athletes experienced this at some point in their careers. There was no magic 'reset' button, but there was a reset process. It has four stages:

1. Write down what is worrying me and why

2. Remind myself why I run and compete

3. Listen to my body and don't push it too hard

4. Remember to never, ever give up

In my heart I knew what was really worrying me, but it took Mike's advice to draw it out. I was scared that I would never achieve anything like the World Marathon Challenge again. Every time someone innocently asked me 'and what next?' those worries would come back.

After a couple of weeks, I managed to let go of these worries and contentment returned. This was helped by doing some training runs and races to prepare for the Manchester Marathon and London Marathon in April.

Always a runner

The joy of running is that it can take us anywhere in the world. It allows us to take on the most varied, and sometimes crazy, challenges.

My heart will always be with road marathons. I love the randomness of the number 26.2 coming to dominate the running community. I love the hardness of the terrain, which allows you to see just how fast you can go. There's no excuses; it's just you and the road. I will still continue to push myself off-road several times a year, though. Losing a whole day running 100 kilometres or further on trails and paths is a wonderful way to clear the mind – it is my 'reset' button.

My only rule is that under no circumstances will I ever camp: I simply cannot abide it. I would rather keep running for a whole week than be forced to camp during an event.

When I am not running, I feel privileged to be able to talk about running – and, I hope, to show other people that what I did is something that anyone can do if they really want to. None of us start out as runners; we make ourselves runners. Whether we become parkrun runners or marathon runners, and whether we take part in local races on a Sunday morning or the Olympics, we are all just runners.

My favourite thing in the world is to be called a runner: it feels like such a privilege. My greatest hope is that I will always be able to call myself a runner.

The World Marathon Challenge results for 2019 are available at: https://worldmarathonchallenge.com/results

Appendix One
Susannah's 21-week Training Programme

Training Programme

Speeds are set as follows:

- Easy running 70% of race pace for 10km

- Medium running 80% of race pace for 10km

- Tempo running 80-90% of race pace for 10km

- Hard running 90% of race pace for 10km

- Cool down running at the end of sessions 60% of race pace for 10km

- Marathon pace that can be maintained over a longer distance (half marathon distance or more)

Running School sessions focused on running technique, strength work, mobility exercises and, when needed, physio sessions to aid recovery. These varied from week-to-week depending on what else was in the training programme.

Strength sessions consisted of upper and lower body exercises. Exact exercises will vary from person to person. It is best to seek advice from a qualified personal trainer or professional as to what will work best for you.

Week 1-4	Monday	Tuesday	Wednesday	Thursday	Friday	Saturday	Sunday	Total running/ walking time
1	**Walk:** 20 minutes **Run:** 15 minutes (easy)	**Run:** 40 minutes *Strength work:* Lower body • squats • straight leg deadlift Upper body • overhead shoulder press • bent over reverse flies • bicep and tricep curls	**Run:** 20 minutes *Intervals:* • Run 1 × 6 minutes • Run 1 × 9 minutes • Run 1 × 6 minutes • Run 1 × 6 minutes (3-minute recovery after each) **Run:** 10 minutes (cool down) Total running time: 69 minutes	Running School session	**Run:** 25 minutes (easy) *Intervals:* • 5 × 1,000m (hard) (3-minute easy run after each) Total running time: 63 minutes (based on 4:30 for 5 × 1,000m pieces)	**Run:** 60 minutes (easy)	**Run/walk for 3 hours:** Run 30 minutes, walk 6 minutes (× 5)	447 minutes (7 hours 27 minutes)
2	**Walk:** 15 minutes **Run:** 25 minutes (easy)	**Run:** 40 minutes (easy) Strength work	**Run:** 20 minutes (warm up) *Intervals:* • 10 × 800m (timed) **Run:** 10 minutes (cool down) Total running time: 70 minutes (based on 4 minute 800m pieces)	Running School session	**Run:** 15 minutes (easy) *Intervals:* • Run 5 minutes fast, 2 minutes easy (× 10) **Run:** 15 minutes (easy) Total running time: 100 minutes	**Run:** 60 minutes (easy)	**Run:** 20 minutes (easy) *Intervals:* • Run 5 × 60 seconds (hard) • Run 5 × 45 seconds (hard) • Run 5 × 30 seconds (hard) (60 seconds recovery between each) **Run:** 60 minutes (easy) Total running time: 92 minutes	402 minutes (6 hours, 42 minutes)

3	**Run:** 30 minutes (easy)	**Run:** 40 minutes (medium) Strength work	**Run:** 20 minutes (easy), 40 minutes (marathon pace) **Run:** 10 minutes (cool down) Total running time: 70 minutes	Running School session	**Run:** 20 minutes (easy) *Intervals:* Run 10 × 1,000m (3-minute jog after each) **Run:** 10-minute (cool down) Total running time: 105 minutes (based on 4:30 minute 1,000m pieces)	Wimbledon Marathon: 3:35	**Run:** 13 miles, half marathon race test time (100 minutes/1 hour 40 minutes) Total running time: 100 minutes	540 minutes (9 hours, 20 minutes)
4	**Run:** 30 minutes (easy)	Strength work	**Run:** 45 minutes (easy)	Running School session	**Run:** 45 minutes (medium)	**Run:** 45 minutes (medium)	**Run for 3 hours:** 30 minutes (easy), 60 minutes (marathon pace), 30 minutes (easy), 60 minutes (marathon pace)	345 minutes (5 hours, 45 minutes)

Week 5–8	Monday	Tuesday	Wednesday	Thursday	Friday	Saturday	Sunday	Total running/ walking time
5	**Walk:** 15 minutes **Run:** 45 minutes (easy)	Strength work	**Run:** 15 minutes (warm up) Intervals: 20 x 90 second sprints (90 seconds recovery walking after each) **Run:** 10 minutes (cool down) Total running/walking time: 85 minutes	Running School session	**Run:** 40 minutes (easy) Intervals: 6 x 1,200m (3 minutes walking after each) **Run:** 10 minutes (cool down) Total running/walking time: 98 minutes (based on 5-minute 1,200m pieces)	**Run for** 90 minutes: 30 minutes (easy), 30 minutes (medium), 30 minutes (marathon pace)	Sussex Marathon: 3:39	552 minutes (9 hours, 12 minutes)
6	**Walk:** 15 minutes **Run:** 45 minutes (easy)	**Run:** 40 minutes (easy) Strength work	**Run:** 20 minutes (warm up) Intervals: 20 x 1-minute hill runs (90 seconds recovery walking after each) **Run:** 10 minutes (cool down) Total running time: 80 minutes	Running School session	**Run:** 40 minutes (easy) Intervals: 6 x 1,200m (1-minute walking recovery after each) **Run:** 10 minutes (cool down) Total running/walking time: 86 minutes (based on 5-minute 1,200m pieces)	**Run:** 60 minutes (easy)	**Run/walk:** 4 hours. Run 40 minutes (easy) walk 5 minutes (x 4)	566 minutes (9 hours, 26 minutes)

7	**Walk:** 15 minutes **Run:** 60 minutes (easy)	Strength work	**Run:** 20 minutes (warm up) *Intervals:* 8 × 4 minutes (hard) (4 minutes jog recovery after each) **Run:** 10 minutes (cool down) Total running time: 94 minutes	Running School session	**Run** for 90 minutes: 30 minutes (easy), 30 minutes (medium), 30 minutes (marathon pace)	**Run** for 90 minutes: 30 minutes (easy), 30 minutes (medium), 30 minutes (marathon pace)	Abingdon Marathon: 3:09
							538 minutes (8 hours, 58 minutes)
8	**Walk:** 20 minutes **Run:** 75 minutes (easy)	Strength work	**Run:** 30 minutes (easy) *Intervals:* 20 × 1-minute runs (90 seconds walking recovery after each) **Run:** 20 minutes (cool down) Total running/walking Time: 100 minutes	Running School session	**Run:** 20 minutes (easy) *Intervals:* 20 × 1 minutes (2-minute jog recovery after each) **Run:** 10 minutes (cool down) Total running/walking time: 90 minutes	Beachy Head Marathon: 3:52	Wimbledon Half Marathon: 1:34
							651 minutes (10 hours, 51 minutes)

Week 9–12	Monday	Tuesday	Wednesday	Thursday	Friday	Saturday	Sunday	Total running/walking time
9	**Walk:** 15 minutes **Run:** 45 minutes (easy)	Strength work:	**Run:** 15 minutes (warm up) *Intervals:* 20 × 90 second (90 seconds walking recovery after each) **Run:** 10 minutes (cool down) Total running/walking time: 85 minutes	Running School session	**Run** for 90 minutes: 30 minutes (easy), 30 minutes (medium), 30 minutes (marathon pace) Total running time: 90 minutes	Thames Path Marathon: 3:17	Marlow Half Marathon: 1:47	539 minutes (8 hours, 59 minutes)
10	**Walk:** 15 minutes **Run:** 45 minutes (easy)	**Run:** 90 minutes Strength work	**Run:** 20 minutes *Intervals:* 20 × 1-minute hill runs (90 seconds recovery walking after each) **Run:** 10 minutes (cool down) Total running/walking time: 80 minutes	Running School session and physio	**Run:** 40 minutes (easy) *Intervals:* 6 × 1,200m (3 minutes walking recovery after each) **Run:** 10 minutes (cool down) Total running/walking time: 98 minutes (based on 5 minute 1,200m pieces)	**Run:** 3 hours (marathon pace)	**Run:** 4 hours (marathon pace)	658 minutes (10 hours, 58 minutes)

Week								Total
11	Run: 90 minutes (easy) Swim: 30 minutes (evening)	Strength work	Run: 30 minutes (easy) Intervals: 8 × 4 minutes (hard) (4 minutes jog recovery after each) Run: 10 minutes (cool down) Total running time: 104 minutes	Running School session and physio	Run for 90 minutes: 30 minutes (easy), 30 minutes (medium), 30 minutes (marathon pace)	Sunset Marathon: 3:52	Run for 90 minutes: 30 minutes (easy), 30 minutes (medium), 30 minutes (marathon pace)	606 minutes (10 hours, 6 minutes)
12	Walk: 20 minutes Run: 75 minutes (easy)	Run: 40 minutes (easy) Strength work	Run: 30 minutes (easy) Intervals: 20 × 1-minute hill sprints (90 seconds walking recovery after each) Run: 20 minutes (cool down) Total running/walking time: 100 minutes	Rest day	Run: 20 minutes (warm up) Intervals: 20 × 1 minute (2 minutes recovery jog after each) Run: 10 minutes (cool down) Total running time: 90 minutes	Run: 13 miles (100 minutes/1:40)	Owler Marathon: 3:37	641 minutes (10 hours, 41 minutes)

Week 13–16	Monday	Tuesday	Wednesday	Thursday	Friday	Saturday	Sunday	Total running/ walking time
13	**Walk:** 15 minutes **Run:** 45 minutes (easy)	Running School session	**Run:** 90 minutes (easy)	**Run:** 60 minutes (medium)	**Run for 2 hours:** 60 minutes (easy), 30 minutes (medium), 30 minutes (marathon pace)	**Run:** 3 hours (marathon pace)	Oulton Park Marathon: 3:39	720 minutes (12 hours, 9 minutes)
14	**Walk:** 20 minutes **Swim:** 45 minutes	**Run:** 90 minutes (easy) Strength work	**Run:** 20 minutes (easy) Intervals: 20 × 1-minute hill runs (90 seconds walking recovery after each) **Run:** 10 minutes (cool down) Total running time: 80 minutes	**Walk:** 30 minutes	Running School session	**Run:** 3 hours (marathon pace)	**Run:** 4 hours (marathon pace)	640 minutes (10 hours, 40 minutes)
15	**Walk:** 20 minutes **Swim:** 45 minutes	Strength work	**Run:** 30 minutes (easy) Intervals: 8 × 4 minutes (hard) (4 minutes jog recovery after each) **Run:** 10 minutes (cool down) Total running time: 104 minutes	Running School session	**Run for 90 minutes:** 30 minutes (easy), 30 minutes (medium), 30 minutes (marathon pace)	Santa's Little Helpers Marathon: 3:23	**Run:** 4 hours (marathon pace)	657minutes (10 hours, 57 minutes)
16	**Walk:** 20 minutes **Swim:** 30 minutes	Enigma Christmas Cracker Marathon 1: 3:35	Enigma Christmas Cracker Marathon 2: 3:28	Running School recovery session	Rest day	**Run:** 4 hours (marathon pace)	12 Days of Christmas Marathon (same course as Santa's Little Helpers): 3:35	898 minutes (14 hours, 58 minutes)

Week 17–21	Monday	Tuesday	Wednesday	Thursday	Friday	Saturday	Sunday	Total running/walking time
17	Easy day - walking 30 minutes	**Run:** 45 minutes (easy)	**Run:** 60 minutes (steady)	**Walk:** 60 minutes	**Run** for 2 hours: 60 minutes (easy), 30 minutes (medium), 30 minutes (marathon pace)	**Run:** 40 minutes *Intervals:* 20 × 1-minute hill runs (90 seconds walking recovery after each) **Run:** 10 minutes (cool down) Total running time: 100 minutes	**Run:** 45 minutes (easy)	460 minutes (7 hours, 40 minutes)
18	**Run:** 60 minutes (easy)	New Year's Day Marathon at Dymchurch: 3:38	**Run:** 20 minutes *Intervals:* 20 × 1-minute hill runs (90 seconds walking recovery after each) **Run:** 10 minutes (cool down) Total running time: 80 minutes	Running School session	**Walk:** 30 minutes	**Run:** 60 minutes *Intervals:* 20 × 1-minute hill sprints (90 seconds recovery after each) **Run:** 10 minutes (cool down) Total running time: 120 minutes	**Run:** 3 hours (marathon pace)	688 minutes (11 hours, 28 minutes)

19	**Walk:** 20 minutes **Swim:** 45 minutes	**Run:** 90 minutes (easy) Strength work	**Walk:** 30 minutes	**Run:** 20 minutes *Intervals:* 20 × 1-minute hill sprints (90 seconds recovery after each) **Run:** 10 minutes (cool down) Total running time: 80 minutes	Running School session	**Run:** 3 hours (marathon pace)	**Run:** 4 hours (marathon pace)	640 minutes (10 hours, 40 minutes)
20	**Walk:** 20 minutes **Swim:** 45 minutes	Strength work	Running School session	**Run:** 30 minutes (easy) *Intervals:* 8 × 4 minutes (hard) (4 minutes walking recovery after each) **Run:** 10 minutes (cool down) Total running time: 104 minutes	**Run** for 90 minutes: 30 minutes (easy), 30 minutes (medium), 30 minutes (marathon pace)	**Run:** 60 minutes *Intervals:* 20 × 1-minute hill sprints (90 seconds recovery after each) **Run:** 10 minutes (cool down) Total running time: 120 minutes	Gloucester Marathon: 3:04	518 minutes (8 hours, 38 minutes)
21	Swim or spin class	Running School session	**Run:** 60 minutes (easy)	**Run:** 20 minutes (easy) *Intervals:* 20 × 90 seconds (hard) (90 seconds walking recovery after each) **Run:** 10 minutes (cool down) Total running time: 90 minutes	**Run:** 20 minutes *Intervals:* 8 × 4 minutes on treadmill (4 minutes walking recovery after each) **Run:** 10 minutes (cool down) Total running time: 94 minutes	**Run:** 60 minutes (easy)	**Run:** 2 hours (steady)	424 minutes (7 hours, 4 minutes)

Appendix Two
Susannah's Warm-up Routine

1. **Skipping** – picking feet up high.

2. **Skipping** – while rotating arms forwards.

3. **Skipping** – while rotating arms backwards.

4. **Skipping** – with knees crossing the centre line of the body.

5. **Side steps:** To open up the hips, step sideways with slightly bent legs, keeping feet straight in front of you. Do ten steps one way and ten steps the other so both legs lead.

6. **All-over body stretches:**

- Hands to opposite feet with straight legs – twist and look to the sky.

- Standing quad stretch – holding one foot at a time.

- Standing glute stretch – place foot into groin push on inside of knee to feel stretch.

- Hamstring and calf stretch – place heel on floor and raise toes, one leg at a time.

- Ankles – rotate each clockwise and anti-clockwise a few times.

- Upper body – place arm across body and pull with the opposite arm to stretch shoulders, then hand behind head and pull with opposite arm to stretch triceps. Rotate arms in opposite directions a few times.

7. **Stretch hip flexors:** Using a knee-high bench or step, place one foot on the object and stretch forwards with leg on bench straight and leg on floor straight. Rotate upper body around bent leg to deepen the stretch.

8. **Glute activations:** Take a step forward diagonally, lean forward from hip with straight back until glutes and hamstring feel engaged. Hold for three seconds and return to vertical position. Repeat ten times on each side.

9. **Body rotation twists:** Place right foot across left, keeping both feet facing forward. Then twist from waist left and right a few times. Then place left foot across right foot and repeat.

10. **Twenty heel flicks**, a deep breath and a big smile to finish.

Appendix Three
Kit List

Packing for seven marathons on seven continents in seven days was stressful. I dreaded arriving at a destination – particularly Antarctica – without the kit I needed.

To help any runners who do the World Marathon Challenge, I've shared what I packed. You may have other things that you like to wear, eat and use when running. I've also listed a couple of things that I did not take but wished I had!

For Antarctica (from head down)

To run in

- Polarised sunglasses
- Thick headband (most people wore hats, but I find my head gets too hot)
- Buff for around the neck (useful for keeping your face warm when the wind gets up)
- Sports bra (girls only!)
- Long-sleeved lightweight tech top
- Running vest

- Leggings (high-waisted styles keep the cold air from getting in)

- Lightweight pair of loose running shorts (wear over leggings to keep glutes warm)

- Pair of knee-high socks

- Pair of ankle length socks (second layer to keep feet warm)

- Pair of trail shoes (more grip than road shoes but still breathable, preventing excess sweat cooling on skin)

- Gloves

To keep warm in

- Woolly hat

- Thick fleece

- Ski jacket

- Ski trousers (warm tracksuit bottoms would be fine and take up less space)

- Foot- and hand-warmers for after the race

- Thick gloves

- A second pair of shoes for after the race to keep feet warm and dry

For the other six marathons (from head down)

- 6 thick headbands

- 6 sports bras

- 6 running vests (you may want a mix of short and long sleeves for day and night runs)

- 6 pairs of running shorts

- 6 pairs of thick running socks

- 2 pairs of running shoes (you may want to pack a third pair in a slightly bigger size)

- Head torch (might be needed for night-time runs)

Like some other female runners, I do not wear knickers underneath my running shorts, as they don't sit comfortably and increase my chance of getting sore. Each to their own on this one!

For travelling between races

- Second pair of leggings for keeping warm (which I used after Antarctica marathon)

- Compression tights (which I used after Madrid marathon for a few hours when my legs felt tired)

- 3 long-sleeved tops

- 4 T-shirts

- 2 zip-up running tops

- Warm hoodie

- 2 pairs of tracksuit bottoms

- Pair of shorts

- 6 pairs of thinner socks

- Underwear

- Pair of flip-flops or any non-trainer shoes to walk in

Other kit

- Rucksack for hand luggage

- 7 labelled bags (plastic or drawstring) for each set of marathon kit (easy to grab the kit you need for each race, helps keep it away from damp and sweaty worn kit)

- Towel (no towels were provided in Perth and Madrid)

- MP3 player

- Chargers for phone, tablet, laptop, MP3 player

- Power adaptors

- Travel neck support (useful for sleeping on flights)

- Toothbrush, small toothpaste and moisturiser in hand luggage (it's so nice to clean your teeth before or after sleeping)

- Currencies as needed (although you can pay for food at the airport on your card)

Medical items

- Paracetamol

- Ibuprofen (but never take much if you're dehydrated – it's bad for the liver)

- Sun cream (factor 50 for Antarctica)

- Savlon (for rubs and sores)

- Nail brush (keeping feet and nails really clean helps prevent sore points and blisters getting infected)

- Plasters

- Small pair of scissors

- Washbag with shampoo, shower gel, deodorant etc.

Food

The food on the plane was good and snacks were available throughout the flight, but I still found myself hungry. It was also nice to have food that I would normally eat between runs:

- Cereal bars (for snacking on)

- Chocolate (for more snacking on: I took 12 Toffee Crisps but ended up buying 6 chocolate bars in Cape Town)

- Marmite

- Peanut butter

- Decaf teabags (mixed with plenty of caffeinated cups of tea)

Things I wish I had taken

- **Foam roller** (a short one that can be attached to a rucksack). This is incredibly useful for easing tight hamstrings, which every runner gets. I was lucky that Kristina lent me hers.

- **Pot Noodles** (or other food to heat and hydrate). Most of us get sick of snacking on sweet and cold food all the time. We had access to hot water on the plane and after each marathon, so I could have taken a few Pot Noodles or other hot food that could be rehydrated. Even the most basic hot food is more comforting and nourishing than yet another cereal bar.

Acknowledgements

First, I thank my coach and co-author Mike Antoniades: none of this would have happened without you. I may have crawled the World Marathon Challenge, but it would not have been a story worth telling.

In a similar vein, I thank the whole team at The Running School for looking after me so meticulously. From sprint sessions and strength work to massages and acupuncture, you've kept me in remarkably good shape despite my own best efforts.

To my family, I am deeply grateful for the support you have always shown and for making me laugh. To Ed, thank you for putting up with me and for your willingness to show interest in the minutiae of my training programme and in writing this book.

A huge thank you to my work colleagues, who showed incredible support throughout. I'm proud to be part of such a fantastic and generous team.

I am enormously grateful to every person who donated to SportsAid and supported the next generation of British sports stars.

I would also like to thank Eve, Laura and the team at Rethink for their invaluable advice and support in shaping my thoughts into a proper book.

My final thank you has to go to the World Marathon Challenge. My fellow runners, race organiser Richard Donovan and the rest of the support team made it a truly unique and amazing experience. Who knew that running around the world could change your own world forever? It certainly did for me.

The Authors

Susannah Gill

Susannah is the female World Record Holder for running seven marathons on seven continents in seven days.

She completed the feat when taking part in the World Marathon Challenge in February 2019, which saw her run 295 kilometres (183 miles) and travel 55,000 miles in 168 hours. She finished six of the seven marathons in first place, with an average race time of 3:28:09, which smashed the previous record of 3:55. She raised nearly £20,000 for SportsAid, a charity that supports Great Britain's next generation of athletes.

Susannah's best marathon time is 2:56, which she achieved at the Manchester Marathon in April 2019. At the 2012 London Marathon she set a Guinness World Record for the fastest woman dressed as an animal, completing the race in a time of 3:18 dressed as a peacock – only to be beaten by a tortoise a few years later.

Aside from the 60+ marathons she has completed over the last decade, Susannah has run numerous ultramarathons, including 100-kilometre, 100-mile and 24-hour races. She is a qualified personal trainer alongside her full-time job as Director of Communications and Corporate Affairs for UK Tote Group. She has worked in horseracing, betting and politics since graduating from the University of Exeter with a degree in history in 2006.

Through her website – www.wecanbeamazing.com – Susannah wants to inspire others to realise that we can all be amazing.

Susannah runs on the streets of London and up and down the hills of Shropshire, England.

🐦 @TheIronLadyRuns and @BeAmazingPT
#BeAmazing

📷 beamazing_personaltraining

Ⓜ info@beamazingpt.co.uk

🌐 www.wecanbeamazing.com

Mike Antoniades

 Mike's passion for rehabilitation and speed began when as a teenager he had a serious anterior cruciate ligament (ACL) injury. After years of bad advice and inefficient rehabilitation, he began to study movement patterns and training methodologies from different sports. He specialised in movement re-patterning and rehabilitation after injury or surgery and focused on speed training for athletes in different sports. For over twenty years, speed and rehabilitation was his hobby. He combined full-time jobs in IT with evenings and weekends training with teams and athletes.

He set up his first Speed company in the UK in 1994, and the first Speed and Rehabilitation centre in 1999. His clients include athletes and teams from the English Premiership, English Championship, German Bundesliga Rugby Union, Rugby league, handball, lacrosse, European Olympic Associations and elite track and field athletes, including world and Olympic gold medallists.

Mike began coaching in 1980, and has worked in the UK, Europe and the USA. He has coached at professional and academy level and is a consultant for professional football clubs and athletes in the UK and Europe. His movement re-patterning methodology is not restricted to elite and up-and-coming athletes: half of all the clients at his two London centres come for rehabilitation after surgery or injury. Mike and his team work successfully with stroke survivors and people with Parkinson's, multiple sclerosis (MS) and other neurological issues.

Mike runs education courses and workshops for coaches, medical practitioners and rehabilitation specialists. He has been described as one of the UK's most innovative coaches and rehabilitation specialists. The Movement & Running School methodology has been rolled out to over forty organisations and franchises in the UK, Germany, Norway, Spain, the Middle East, Japan and the US.

He has been featured on TV in the UK, Europe and in the US and in newspapers and magazines for his work with children's movement, running and elite athletes.

𝕏 @MikeAntoniades @RunningSchool

▣ therunningschool

Ⓜ run@runningschool.co.uk

⊕ www.runningschool.com